Practically RAW

Flexible Raw Recipes Anyone Can Make

Amber Shea Crawley

with a foreword by Matthew Kenney

VEGAN HERITAGE PRESS

Woodstock • Virginia

Practically Raw: Flexible Raw Recipes Anyone Can Make by Amber Shea Crawley
(Copyright © 2012 by Amber Shea Crawley)

Printed in the United States of America
10 9 8 7 6 5 4 3 2

ISBN 13: 978-0-9800131-5-3
ISBN 10: 0-9800131-5-1

Vegan Heritage Press books are available at quantity discounts. For information, please visit our website at www.veganheritagepress.com or write the publisher at Vegan Heritage Press, P.O. Box 628, Woodstock, VA 22664-0628.

Library of Congress Cataloging-in-Publication Data
Crawley, Amber Shea, 1985-
  Practically raw : flexible raw recipes anyone can make / Amber Shea Crawley. -- 1st ed.
    p. cm.
  Includes index.
  ISBN 978-0-9800131-5-3
  1. Cooking (Natural foods) 2. Raw foods. 3. Cookbooks. I. Title.
TX741.C73 2012
641.3'02--dc23
                    2011041844

Cover photos: Photo of the author by Stephen Melvin. Food photos by Amber Shea Crawley: (clockwise from bottom) Almond Butter Sesame Noodles, 141; Parisian Street Crepes, page 61; Mushroom Nut Burgers, page 144. **Interior photos:** photos of the author by Stephen Melvin; food photos by Amber Shea Crawley. Spot illustrations of individual ingredients from stock photo sources.

Disclaimer: The information provided in this book should not be taken as medical advice. If you require a medical diagnosis or prescription, or if you are contemplating any major dietary change, please consult a qualified health-care provider. You should always seek an expert medical opinion before making changes in your diet or supplementation regimen.

Publisher's Note: The information in this book is correct and complete to the best of our knowledge. Website addresses and contact information were correct at the time of publication. The publisher is not responsible for specific health or allergy issues or adverse reactions to recipes contained in this book.

Dedication

To Matt,
for all the love, laughter, and encouragement a girl
could ask for, and

To my parents,
for a lifetime of support and believing in me.

Contents

Foreword

When I was first introduced to it many years ago, raw food was a relatively unknown lifestyle practiced by a few niche groups around the country. This was before the days of its brief cameo on *Sex and the City,* or the laser focus it began to receive from celebrities in recent years. While the health benefits of raw were quite well explained even in those early days, the quality of the cuisine itself had a long way to go. It was mostly being prepared by untrained and self-taught chefs, and while the food could be satisfying on some levels, the true potential of raw cuisine remained untapped. Most of my early raw meals were centered on nut-heavy, often labor-intensive preparations that, in the end, filled me more than satisfied me. And yet, they were good enough that I almost instantly felt better both physically and mentally.

I envisioned raw food on a larger stage, one that would allow people to eat healthfully while still enjoying the wonders of gourmet cuisine. Cookbooks on the subject were few and far between, and those that did exist were not particularly helpful in guiding me toward the wonderful food I imagined. I think of those searching days with fondness, even as I recall cracking coconuts with an ax in my yard before attempting a curried coconut soup. Upon announcing the opening of a high-end raw food restaurant in New York City, I found the skeptics out in full force. When a couple of early diners, and even one potential employee, expressed that they could only work or eat while barefoot (to be more "grounded"), I began to worry that this chosen mission may have been too challenging to convey to a broader, more mainstream audience. Still, my partners and I persisted in working diligently to show that raw food could be vibrant and delicious. New inroads were made as more and more people began to incorporate raw into their daily lives. They became healthier and learned that they could still enjoy dinner while doing so.

Along with my goal of helping to spread the word about the wonders of eating a plant-based diet, I also believe in educating chefs about creating healthier choices. The world will be a much better place when we finally realize the connection between food and health. Launching the Matthew Kenney Academy, an upscale culinary institute emphasizing contemporary raw food, seemed like the perfect way for me to embark on this mission. This was an even greater stretch of the imagination than opening a niche restaurant in New York. The location I chose for this high-end, raw-only school wasn't New York, however, but Oklahoma, a true meat-and-potatoes state. It was there that I first met the wonderfully talented Amber Shea Crawley.

Upon our first email contact, I was immediately charmed by Amber's writing style—precise and articulate, while still warm and conversational. I could not have been more pleased when she decided to follow her passion for healthier cuisine by joining our Academy. We all benefited from her decision. As a founder of the Academy, I feel extremely honored that Amber is our first graduate to author her own cookbook.

Practically Raw is a mature first book, presenting raw and healthy vegan food as approachable and tasty, as opposed to challenging and rigid. The recipes, which provide both raw and cooked options, are simply brilliant, and her book focuses on many healthier versions of the foods we all love. Flexibility is not a concept historically associated with raw cuisine, and yet Amber both embraces and encourages it. A plant-based diet is far from rigid—in fact, it is the most abundant and beautiful way to eat. We just need to follow Amber's advice and take it all with a "grain of salt." In other words, you need not have a panic attack if the almonds in your arugula salad have been roasted or if there are a few tablespoons of maple syrup in a dessert.

You will be inspired to create Amber's recipes in your own kitchen. *Practically Raw* is not only a cookbook, but also a handbook that will help you understand the why and how of successfully living a plant-based lifestyle. Along with fun and delicious recipes, the book offers many hidden nuggets of information, all explained in the same comfortable tone that Amber so easily communicates. While *Practically Raw* is easy to use and offers flexibility with its recipes, it also offers a refreshingly new perspective on what a cookbook is all about. In addition to a fabulous selection of soups, salads, entrées, and dessert recipes, Amber has boldly redefined our expectations, with full chapters devoted to foods she loves, such as delicious and addictive kale chips, unique hummus preparations and, for those who can't decide which wonderful recipes to make first, well-balanced meal plans. The result is an original book that is not only practical, but also fun and user-friendly.

As an educator and someone who spends the majority of my life working to improve the food that we eat each day, I am especially grateful that Amber is sharing her culinary vision in this exciting cookbook. For anyone wanting to become more comfortable and familiar with the charms and benefits of a plant-based diet, look no further than *Practically Raw.*

—Matthew Kenney, founder of the Matthew Kenney Academy

Introduction

Practically Raw is unlike any other cookbook on the market today. Not only can the raw, vegan recipes it contains be made with or without special equipment and ingredients, but the option is also given to cook or bake the dishes instead of preparing them raw. It's the first flexible raw food recipe book that will appeal to seasoned raw foodists, newbies to raw or vegan food, home cooks short on time or money, and anyone who appreciates flexible recipes for delicious, vibrant, healthful, sexy food. Whether the reader is exploring raw food because of an interest in health and longevity, a food allergy or chronic illness, a desire to lose weight, or ethical or environmental concerns, *Practically Raw* has something for everybody.

As a raw food chef and nutritionist, my objective is twofold: to delight your taste buds and nourish your body with some of the most healthful and delicious foods on the planet—raw and living foods. My job is a little more complicated than that, though, because in fulfilling those goals I must also keep in mind a number of other factors such as preparation time, budget, experience level, ingredient availability, access to specialized equipment, and more. Let's face it—this is the real world, and when it comes to food, the affordability, convenience, and ease of preparation of a dish are often just as important as nutrition and taste.

Along the way, I have no intention of trying to convince you to be 100 percent raw or vegan—my book is a judgment-free zone. Instead, I want to meld my love for beautiful, gourmet raw cuisine with my practical, flexible approach to diet. If you're like me, you want to avoid treating food or diet like a religion or, perhaps worse, an inflexible daily duty. Instead, let's focus on food as a source of nourishment and enjoyment, two positive and universal desires, and aspire to fuel our bodies to the best (and yummiest) of our abilities.

The recipes in this book are designed to allow you to choose the degree to which you incorporate raw foods into your life. You can dip your toes into the world of raw, or you can dive in headfirst—the choice is yours. To this end, *Practically Raw* is the first raw food recipe book to offer you the luxury of choice, every step of the way. Can't find (or afford) a certain ingredient? I tell you what you can substitute and even what you can leave out. You don't have a dehydrator? No problem. I provide directions on how to bake or cook each item. You choose the pace at which you want to "go raw," and I'll be there to help you.

It is my hope that this book will appeal to a large audience across a wide spectrum of foodies. It provides brand new recipes and creative ideas to seasoned raw foodists, as well as guidance and easy-to-digest information to the raw food newbie. It also offers flexible meal ideas, shortcuts, and substitutions to the hurried home cook on a budget. You'll also find nutrition data and lifestyle tips. For more information, ideas, and discussion, please always feel free to visit me at almostveganchef.com. Relax, have fun, and enjoy the journey.

If you do have experience with raw foods, then I'm equally eager to introduce you to these mouthwatering and exciting new recipes. Some recipes take longer to make than others, and some will be fancier than others, but which recipes you make and how "raw" you choose to prepare them are completely up to you. No matter who you are or what your background, I want to help you achieve optimum health, heal your body, trim down, and ultimately change your life in easy, convenient, and manageable ways using raw and living foods. I promise to be your guide every step of the way—follow me.

Raw, Practically

I adore raw food and include a great deal of it in my diet year-round. Eating plenty of fresh fruits and vegetables and nutritious nuts and seeds makes me feel energetic, vibrant, and alive. That said, I have a confession to make: my diet is not 100 percent raw, and I'm okay with that!

If you are like me, you may feel your best when you balance raw foods in your diet with healthful and satisfying cooked foods. I say go for it! You are welcome to embrace raw food to any degree of your choosing, and you are also free to vary your raw food intake from day to day or season to season. That's what I do, and that's why I call my diet *Practically Raw*.

What Does "Practically Raw" Mean to Me?

Well, let's start with the word "practically."

prac·ti·cal·ly/' praktik(ə)lē / adverb

1. Virtually; almost.
2. In a practical manner.

As a linguist, I love the double entendre of "practically," and both definitions fit my philosophy perfectly. First, "practically raw" means "almost raw," representing my belief in substituting non-raw ingredients or using non-raw cooking techniques when desired or warranted. It means that "raw" does not have to be an all-or-nothing affair.

For instance, I will sometimes add a cooked ingredient to an otherwise raw dish, like throwing a handful of black beans into a raw taco filling or including cooked edamame in a raw stir-fry. I also have no problem replacing raw ingredients with non-raw counterparts, such as storebought nondairy milk instead of homemade almond milk or cooked whole grain noodles in place of spiralized zucchini pasta, when it's convenient and practical for me to do so. Sometimes I even divide up a recipe, making some of it raw and some of it not; for example, I might send most of a batch of kale chips to the dehydrator to dry overnight, but I'll reserve one serving and bake it for myself right then as an instant-gratification snack.

Practically Raw means that it is okay to sometimes step outside the boundaries of raw, and I even encourage it when it is practical to do so. It means that even if your access to truly raw ingredients or special equipment is limited, you can still utilize what's available to emulate raw food dishes. I think it's perfectly fine to use roasted tahini instead of raw in your hummus, for instance, or to bake up flax crackers in the oven instead of dehydrating them.

Practically Raw also applies to time considerations. Let's say you planned to dehydrate a dish overnight, but you just found out that company's arriving in two hours; in that case, you may make the practical decision to bake it instead. In all these cases, you'll end up with an incredibly nutritious meal, and though it may not be all raw or "technically" raw, it's still a whole foods meal made entirely of natural, unprocessed ingredients.

In short: to be *Practically Raw* is to be flexible. (This is not, however, the same as being "flexitarian," a term that refers to someone who has cut down on their meat consumption but still eats animals occasionally.) When I call myself "flexible," it means I consider all recipes, including (and especially) my own, to be adjustable, adaptable, and amenable to modifications.

My Journey to Veganism and Raw Food

When I was in college, I lost some excess weight by employing a low-calorie, low-fat diet and a daily exercise plan. After that, I was officially hooked on health. However, health, insofar as diet is concerned, means something very different to me now than it did back then. My forays into low-cal eating had me avoiding high-fat animal products (like red meat and cheese), of which I'd never been a fan even as a child. During that time, I did consume foods such as skim milk, chicken, and egg substitutes, but I was also introduced to vegetarian meat analogs and soymilk around the same time, so I incorporated those as well. As I acquired more nutrition knowledge, I found myself eating fewer processed foods and less meat and dairy of any kind, eventually to the point where I realized I was only eating chicken once or twice a month at most, and hardly any dairy whatsoever. At that moment, I decided to cut it out for good and start thinking of myself as a vegan.

Within a few months, I was training for my first marathon and feeling slimmer, more fit, and more energetic than ever. I was soon inspired to create a weblog to share my way of eating with the world. I wanted a way to combine my love for writing (my bachelor's degree is in linguistics) with my passion for nutrition and healthy food. In August 2008, my blog, Almost Vegan (almostveganchef.com), was born.

Why did I call my blog "almost" vegan? The fact is, I eat a vegan diet primarily for health reasons, both physical and mental, and to not contribute to animal suffering, but I'm not a fan of strict or dogmatic "rules" about food. I prefer to be flexible and focus on enjoying what I eat. I think people can sometimes set themselves up for failure if they insist on being "perfect", and I find I'm psychologically healthier and happier if I don't "forbid" myself to have any particular type of food. My blog is the embodiment of this philosophy.

Blogging accelerated my journey to maximum health more than anything, even losing weight. I was constantly being introduced to new foods, recipes, and ideas through the vegan blogosphere, and it wasn't long before raw foodism appeared on my radar. At first, I couldn't understand why anyone would prohibit themselves from eating a hot meal, or beans, or tofu. Soon, though, it clicked for me: there's no rule that says you have to eat all raw to be a part of the movement! I realized that raw foodism doesn't have to be all-or-nothing. I began slowly, trying raw items at a few restaurants and preparing some raw snacks and desserts at home. Everything tasted pretty good, but I still wasn't convinced that raw food was for me.

My "aha" moment came in 2010, when my then-boyfriend (now husband) Matt and I took a Memorial Day weekend road trip to Dallas, Texas. On our way south from Kansas City, we stopped at a raw restaurant in Oklahoma City called Matthew Kenney OKC (formerly known as 105degrees). I'd heard about it from a fellow blogger, and I was excited to try a 100 percent raw meal for the first time. I never expected to be so blown away by the flavor and quality of the food, or to feel so satisfied and deliriously high on life as I did after that lunch. It was then that I knew that raw food was a path I very much wanted to travel.

In the following months I experimented with raw food and developed a secret dream of attending the Matthew Kenney Academy (formerly called the 105degrees Academy). After a great deal of encouragement from Matt, my family, and my blog readers, I took the plunge: I quit my life insurance job of four years and enrolled at the academy.

Culinary school was one of the most amazing experiences of my life. Within a few months, I was a certified living foods chef and was irreversibly, obsessively in love with raw food and how it made me feel. When I returned home, I set to work increasing the web presence of my name and blog. To that end, in February 2011, I nervously entered an online video contest sponsored by the Living Light Culinary Arts Institute, another raw chef school in California. Imagine my surprise when my video for Caramel-Fudge Brownies (page 204) was elected the winner—by a landslide! In May of that year I took advantage of the cash scholarship prize by enrolling in a 103-hour series of intensive nutrition courses at Living Light, graduating as a certified raw food nutrition educator. Finally, I had some credentials to match my rabid, years-long obsession with health and wellness!

The Wonderful World of Raw

Put simply, a raw vegan diet consists of fruits, vegetables, nuts, and seeds in their natural, unprocessed state, never heated above approximately 118° Fahrenheit (48° Celsius) in order to preserve the full nutritional value (see Cooked vs. Raw on page 12). The benefits of eating raw foods are vast, so whether you're a committed vegan or a meat-and-potatoes omnivore, here are some compelling reasons to consider adding more raw foods to your daily diet.

Raw food has more of what your body wants and less of what it doesn't want. A raw vegan diet is rich in vitamins, minerals, fiber, water, essential fatty acids, plant protein, beneficial enzymes and probiotics, phytochemicals, and antioxidants. It is free of processed sugars, artificial sweeteners, chemicals and preservatives, unhealthy fats, animal products, and common allergens that can include gluten and soy. Also, if you buy organic, a raw diet minimizes your intake of pesticides and genetically modified organisms (GMOs).

Raw food is gentle on your digestion. Have you ever eaten a large, rich meal, only to feel pangs (literally) of regret shortly thereafter? When you overload your system with heavy cooked food (especially meat, dairy, and processed carbohydrates), digestion becomes a laborious task. When you eat raw, however, not only is digestion speedier and more comfortable, but your body is better able to assimilate the unadulterated nutrients the food contains. The fiber and enzymes in raw food also help ease your body's digestive process. A raw diet can be particularly helpful to those with food allergies, intolerances, or sensitivities (such as gluten or soy), as raw food is free of most common allergens.

Raw food is kind to animals and to the planet. A vegan diet is one of the most effective ways to fight animal suffering in today's world. When you shun meat, poultry, fish, eggs, and dairy products, you refuse to support the abuse endured by animals raised for food. A raw diet, free of processed foods, also lessens your participation in the environmental destruction perpetrated by today's industrial agriculture. Such a choice increases the amount of grain available to feed people elsewhere, reduces pollution, saves water and energy, and withdraws your contribution to the clearing of forests for animal farming.

Raw food will send your energy levels through the roof. After an initial detoxification period, when the body is adjusting to a higher intake of pure, nutritious food, most people who transition to a raw diet experience a surge in energy. Don't be surprised when you feed your body more vibrant, live food and you end up feeling more vibrantly alive! The abundance of vitamins and minerals and the lack of empty calories will combine to make you feel lighter, happier, and more energetic. You may even reap the benefits of improved sleep quality, smoother skin, and a sharper memory.

Raw food can help you achieve and/or maintain your ideal weight. Fresh fruits and vegetables are low in calories but high in vitamins and minerals. The more produce you include in your daily diet, the less room there will be for your old, unhealthy standbys (which were almost certainly higher-calorie). Better yet, you won't feel deprived, since nuts and seeds contain protein and healthy fats and are extremely filling. Oh, and two words: raw desserts. Yum! Not only will you feel nourished and satisfied, but low-effort weight loss (or maintenance) is more easily attainable.

A great deal of raw food is quick and easy to prepare. No really, it's true! Yes, you can invest in a dehydrator, but it's perfectly possible to thrive on a raw diet without one. Think of how long it takes to peel a banana, throw together a salad, blend a smoothie or grab a handful of nuts...then compare that to the time you might currently spend in the kitchen (or waiting for the pizza man!). Often, in the time it would take you to preheat the oven or boil a pot of water, you can easily prepare a filling, satisfying raw meal or snack. A partially raw diet is full of instant gratification.

Raw foods could help you live a longer, healthier life. A raw diet naturally supports the immune system, decreases inflammation, and floods your body with antioxidants, which deactivate free radicals in the body. As a result, eating raw food can help decrease your susceptibility to common ailments like colds, the flu, and fatigue—as well as to more severe and chronic conditions such as cancer, heart disease, and diabetes. In giving your body better nutrition, you're increasing your own longevity.

You don't have to eat only raw foods to reap these rewards. Eating raw food is not a black-or-white decision, but rather a matter of proportions. Every raw snack, side dish, or meal you add to your day will benefit your body. Simply put: the more raw foods one eats, the better one feels and the longer one is likely to live.

In short, whether you're exploring raw food because of an interest in health and longevity, a nagging food allergy or chronic illness, a desire to lose weight, ethical or environmental concerns, or just curiosity, raw food has a lot to offer you. With rewards like these, you may very well find yourself falling head over heels in love with the raw side of life. No matter what your knowledge level or budget may be, raw food can be for you! I'm here to help you ease into a practically raw lifestyle at whatever pace you choose.

An Evolution in Raw Food Philosophy

"Flexible" is not yet a pervasive buzzword in the raw community, but the seeds of the idea are there, ready to germinate. To start with, most raw foodies have never shied away from making use of certain non-raw ingredients like maple syrup and nutritional yeast. But in just the last couple of years, it's gone beyond that. Scanning scores of blogs, I've observed that many "raw foodists" now admit to including at least some amount of cooked food in their diet. Many members of the community are moving away from a 100 percent raw "ideal" to a more forgiving 80/20-ish mentality. (This is what is meant inside and outside the raw community when they refer to "the 80/20 rule.") So, while it used to be the case that a person was either Raw or Not Raw, I've noticed that people nowadays who are mostly or even halfway raw call themselves "raw foodists." It isn't pure, but it works. So, although "practical" and "flexible" are not yet widely used terms in the raw food world, they are terms for which I believe the raw community is ripe and ready. With a practical, flexible outlook on raw food, even people who are brand new to raw will be able to experiment and indulge their curiosity and newfound enthusiasm to any degree they please—which, to me, is the best possible way to give rise to a passion and a lifestyle shift. In addition, those of you who are already devoted raw foodies might find this flexible, practical approach to be a breath of fresh air which you're ready and eager to inhale.

There is no such thing as "cheating"—only "choosing." This statement summarizes my entire diet philosophy and is the root of the reason I am "practically raw." To me, there is a big difference between "I can't" and "I won't." Instead of declaring that I "can't" have certain foods—a dietary restriction which can invite feelings of deprivation—I prefer to say that I "won't" eat certain foods, which is a dietary decision that makes me feel comfortable and empowered. Eating practically raw is effortless to me because I don't consider my diet to be a law or commandment that I'm constantly in danger of breaking or "cheating" on—instead, it's simply a choice I make each day.

Making Raw Food Quicker, Easier, and Affordable

It's well known that raw food isn't the cheapest of diets. In place of dollar menus and fast-food drive-thrus, a high-raw diet derives its calories from fresh, natural, high-quality, preferably organic fruits, vegetables, nuts, and seeds that you prepare yourself. Needless to say, this can often cost more—in time and in money—than a diet of processed food. Although you should be prepared to shell out a little more dough up front, keep in mind that you'll be paying it forward on all the incredible health benefits you'll soon enjoy.

That said, there are some effective strategies to make raw food more affordable, as well as quicker and easier to prepare. Here is a handy list to refer to whenever you want to strategize the cost and procedures for eating raw food:

- **Buy in bulk.** My favorite way to lower the cost of nuts, seeds, dried fruits, spices, and other shelf-stable items is to buy them in bulk, either at a warehouse store such as Costco, from the bulk bins of a health food store, or from online retailers (see Resources, page 228).

- **Or don't buy in bulk.** I know this contradicts the point above, but on the flipside, avoid buying more than you will use. If you're making a recipe that calls for just 1 rib of celery, for instance, there's no need to buy a whole bunch; just go to your grocery store's salad bar for a few cents' worth of chopped celery. Take advantage of bulk bins in the same way, and only buy as much as you know you'll use.

- **Eat seasonally.** Fresh fruits and vegetables that are in season are often cheaper than out-of-season produce flown in from halfway around the world. Search "produce in season" on Google for lists of what's in season and when.

- **Shop sales, farmers markets, and international grocers.** Along with shopping seasonally, scope out sales fliers for your local stores, and don't miss the unbeatable values available at farmers markets, Asian grocers, and other international food stores.

- **Plan ahead.** Pick out some recipes at the beginning of the week that you'd like to make, then create a schedule for preparing them. Take note of ingredients needed, dehydration times, whether nuts need to be soaked, or if there's any other component recipes you need to make before you tackle your list.

- **Prep in advance.** A couple of hours of food prep early in the week can save many hours later on. Raw dishes often keep well, too, so you can easily make two to three days' worth of food (or more) at a time instead of being in the kitchen every single day.

- **Overdo it.** You can double or triple the recipes you make so that you have enough for lunch, leftovers, or snacks throughout the week.

- **Plant a garden.** I say this having no green thumb myself, but if you enjoy gardening, try growing some of your own fresh fruits, vegetables, and herbs.

- **Sprout.** Read up on how to grow your own sprouts—you can find lots of tutorials online. You don't even need a garden, just a few glass jars and some cheesecloth.

- **Eat raw until dinner.** Breakfast is the easiest meal to eat raw. Have a smoothie, a bowl of granola, or some chia porridge, and you're set! For lunch, I almost always eat leftovers from the night before. A quick-to-make soup or salad is another great lunch option.

- **Keep it simple.** There's no need for every eating occasion to be gourmet. Fresh fruits and vegetables are nature's perfect snack, so indulge in those as often as you please.

- **Substitute, substitute, substitute!** Anytime an expensive or difficult-to-find ingredient is called for, be sure to consider the substitution suggestions at the end of each recipe, as you may find a thriftier or more readily available alternative. Similarly, if a recipe appears to take more time to prepare than you can spare, watch for tips to speed up prep time by cooking or baking.

Nutrition Guide

As I am not a medical or dietary practitioner, the information in this book should not be taken as prescriptive advice. In fact, you should always seek an expert medical opinion before making changes to your diet or supplementation regimen.

However, I credit my passion for nutrition with leading me to embrace veganism and raw foodism. I think it's incredibly important for everyone to have at least a fundamental grasp on human nutrition; however, many people get lost in the jargon and details of nutritional science. My goal here is to give you a basic primer on nutrition without overwhelming you with technicalities. This is in no way an exhaustive explanation of all things nutrition-related—there's much more than can be crammed into these few pages—but it's a great place to start.

Water

Often overlooked, water is one of the most important components of our diet. It makes up 70 percent of our body weight, is found in every one of our cells, tissues, and organs, and is a key actor in almost every bodily function and process. It's extremely important to stay hydrated every day; eight to ten 8-ounce glasses of pure, filtered water per day is a good minimum to aim for. You can also take in extra fluids through food, and raw food is often a fantastic source. Eating plenty of juicy fruits and water-rich fresh vegetables will help keep your body hydrated and happy.

Calories

A calorie is a unit of energy. One kilocalorie (equivalent to one dietary calorie) is the amount of energy needed to increase the temperature of a kilogram of water by 1°C. That sounds complicated, but nutritionally speaking, calories are simply our body's preferred form of fuel, used to power everything from breathing to thinking to exercise.

A person's daily recommended calorie intake depends on a number of factors, including age, sex, height and weight, and activity level. Typically, however, a moderately active woman requires about 2,000 calories per day, with the average man requiring approximately 2,500.

That said, it is usually not necessary to track the exact number of calories you eat. Our bodies are equipped with numerous satiety mechanisms that allow us to intuitively know how much food we require. Sometimes, though, especially after years on a high-calorie, nutrient-poor Standard American Diet, these mechanisms can get thrown out of whack, in which case it can be a good idea to track your calories for a few days and try to recalibrate your body to expect a proper amount of fuel. Dietary calories come from only four sources: proteins, carbohydrates, fats, and alcohol.

Macronutrients

A macronutrient is a chemical compound that provides energy (calories). The preferred source of energy for most of our cells is carbohydrates. After our carb stores are emptied, fat is then utilized. Only after burning up our usable stores of both carbs and fat will the body switch to burning protein (muscle tissue) for energy.

Carbohydrates. Carbohydrates come in numerous forms, but they all contain 4 calories per gram and are derived from plant sources. So-called "simple carbs," found in fruits and various sugars, require little digestion and thus are a quick energy source, while starchy "complex carbs," found in vegetables, grains, and legumes, require more digestion time than simple carbohydrates. Because they are burned in a constant, time-released manner, fiber-rich complex carbohydrates are the body's best source of fuel, as they do not spike blood sugar and can provide sustained physical energy. The bulk of our daily calories—at least 50 percent—ought to come from carbohydrates, emphasizing vegetables and fruits, and limiting added sugars.

Fiber. Though it is a type of carbohydrate, fiber is a non-caloric nutrient, as it passes through our bodies unabsorbed. Fiber is vital to a healthy diet, as it pushes our food through the digestive tract and can also lower cholesterol, decrease the risk of colon cancer, and relieve constipation. You should aim for at least 35 grams daily, but on a raw and vegan diet, I routinely find myself consuming 60-80 grams per day!

Fats. Fats (also called fatty acids or lipids) contain 9 calories per gram and are crucial for energy storage, vitamin and mineral absorption, hormone balance, and cell communication.

Unsaturated fats provide cell membrane fluidity and help transmit nerve impulses. These fats can either be monounsaturated, such as those in olives, olive oil, nuts, and avocados, or polyunsaturated, including the EFAs (essential fatty acids such as omega-3s and -6s) that we must obtain from our diet. Though it's often thought that fish are the best source of the omega-3 fat DHA, our bodies can actually synthesize it from ALA, an omega-3 fat found in flax, hemp, and chia, as well as in small amounts in leafy greens. If you're concerned about your body's ability to convert ALA to DHA, you can take an algae-derived DHA supplement. Omega-6 fats, such as those in

WHY INCLUDE NUTRITIONAL DATA?

Every body is different, and due to this biochemical individuality, there is no such thing as a one-size-fits-all diet. Some people like to eat more protein than average, others prefer less fat or fewer carbohydrates, and still others count their daily calories. Some folks want to lose weight; others want to gain. Sometimes there's a medical issue. For these reasons and more, I wanted to provide the nutritional breakdown for all my recipes.

I've also heard complaints about a raw diet being either too low or too high in calories. With this nutritional information, you'll be able to pick out low- or high-cal recipes as your needs dictate. In addition, you can use the information to combine various dishes into perfectly portioned meals and snacks. For example, after eating a plate of extremely low-calorie, low-fat Spaghetti alla Marinara (page 136) for dinner, you'll know you can indulge in a higher-cal dessert like, say, Cinnamon Crumble Coffee Cakes (page 207) afterward, guilt-free.

seeds and vegetable oils, are essential as well, but they are already quite plentiful in any diet, so it's not necessary to specifically seek them out.

Medium-chain saturated fats, such as those in coconut products, provide stiffness and stability for cell membranes. (Long-chain saturated fats from animal products, however, can have deleterious effects on our cholesterol and heart health). Man-made trans fats, which are created by hydrogenating vegetable oils (in other words, causing polyunsaturated fats to behave like saturated ones) are unnecessary in our diet and dangerous to our cardiovascular system, and should be avoided. Luckily, they are not found in any natural, raw, vegan foods.

Some people worry that a raw food diet is too high in fat, but bear in mind that the type of fat you're consuming tends to matter more than the total number of grams. When your diet is filled with anti-inflammatory omega-3 fatty acids, heart-healthy monounsaturated fats, and antimicrobial medium-chain saturated fats, your body will be able to put all of them to beneficial use, unlike the more sinister long-chain saturated and trans fats. (Also see Cutting the Fat, page 18, and Spotlight on Fats, page 187.)

Protein. Containing 4 calories per gram, protein is in every cell in the body. It comprises 20 percent of our body weight and largely makes up our skin, eyes, nails, hair, brain, heart, blood cells, and immune system cells. Proteins in food are actually long chains of amino acids (which are the building blocks of all proteins) that the body breaks down during digestion. Of the twenty naturally occurring amino acids, eight to ten (depending on whom you ask) are deemed "essential" for humans, as they cannot be made within our bodies and must instead be obtained from food.

Most Americans have grossly inflated notions of our protein needs, when in reality the average daily requirements for adults are 46 and 56 grams for women and men, respectively. Not only is this amount easily obtained through a plant-based diet, but there is such a thing as too much protein. An excess of protein in your diet can stress your kidneys, and numerous epidemiological surveys, such as *The China Study,* have linked high dietary protein intake (particularly of protein from animal sources) with increased risk of cancer. Plant protein is not only healthier, it's also more bioavailable, meaning that it's more easily absorbed by our bodies.

Please don't fret about protein combining or getting "complete proteins" in your diet. Every single food contains a mixture of all the essential amino acids in varying amounts, so as long as you're eating a varied diet and not living exclusively on apples or macadamia nuts, you're getting the essential amino acids you need. Beans and legumes, nuts and seeds, grains and pseudograins, and leafy greens are all excellent sources of protein.

Alcohol. If you choose to include alcohol in your diet, it contains 7 calories per gram, but is not an essential nutrient. I myself enjoy the occasional glass of wine or mixed drink; just be sure not to overdo it, and always drink safely and responsibly.

Micronutrients

Micronutrients are nutrients we require in small quantities to orchestrate many of our bodies' physiological functions.

Vitamins. Vitamins are organic compounds that must be obtained through our diet. They are classified as either fat-soluble (vitamins A, D, E, and K) or water-soluble (all eight B vitamins and vitamin C). Vitamins have diverse functions in the body, including regulation of metabolism and cell and tissue growth. Some vitamins, such as vitamin C, also function as antioxidants. The hardy fat-soluble vitamins are absorbed with the help of lipids (fats) and can be stored in our bodies over time, whereas the more fragile water-soluble vitamins are susceptible to heat damage, and since they dissolve easily in water in our bodies, they are not readily stored.

Vitamins occur in abundance in raw food, especially fresh fruits and vegetables, with the exception of vitamin D (which is best obtained through sunlight) and vitamin B_{12} (which must be supplemented in vegan diets). Some folks think that the absence of B_{12} indicates that a vegan diet is an unsuitable eating style for modern humans, who usually get their B_{12} from animal products. It may surprise you to learn that factory-farmed meat contains B_{12} because the animals are given supplements! Take a short-cut by ingesting a B_{12} supplement yourself.

Minerals. Minerals are elements, so they are derived from the earth and do not break down into smaller compounds. They are important for our nervous system, skeletal system, energy production, and much more. Sodium, calcium, iron, potassium, magnesium, zinc, and selenium are a few of the minerals that must be obtained from our diet. Though most people think of dairy as the best source for calcium, in reality, leafy greens are the calcium kings! Iron, also, is found in more than just animal products—nuts, seeds, and leafy greens all contain it, for instance. Also, plant-based (non-heme) iron is selectively absorbed by our bodies (unlike heme iron found in meat), ensuring that we never store an excess, which can lead to iron toxicity.

Antioxidants. Antioxidants reduce levels of oxidative stress in our bodies by donating an electron to neutralize free radical molecules, which wreak havoc on our cells. Potent antioxidants include vitamin C, vitamin E, resveratrol, lycopene, lutein, zeaxanthin, flavonoids, carotenoids, and many more, each with their own unique set of functions. Many antioxidants are heat-sensitive, so they're best obtained from raw foods. Some people will claim that certain antioxidants, like lycopene in tomatoes, are more bioavailable when cooked, but this is not the case—cooked foods simply contain less water, and therefore more lycopene per gram, than their raw forms. Therefore, it's a matter of concentration, not quality or availability.

As mentioned, this is but a cursory glance at the science of nutrition. There is much more to be said about these topics as well as others, such as phytonutrients, polyphenols, probiotics, plant sterols, and so many more! I highly encourage you to use this information as a springboard to your own investigations into the wonderful world of nutrition.

Cooked vs. Raw

I hope the information provided here has convinced you that a vegan diet is not only nutritionally adequate, but is also one of the simplest and healthiest ways to eat a wide variety of nutrients every day. But why is raw vegan food nutritionally superior to cooked vegan food?

- **Nutrient loss:** Water-soluble vitamins, including vitamin C and all B-complex vitamins, and most antioxidants are susceptible to heat damage and are often lost through the processes of cooking, boiling, grilling, frying, and pasteurization. Think about it: we humans can't survive for very long in an environment that is 118°F or hotter. Similarly, many nutrients can't withstand that much heat, either.

- **Toxins:** Harmful carcinogens and toxins such as advanced glycation endproducts (AGEs), acrylamide, polycyclic aromatic hydrocarbons (PAHs), heterocyclic amines, and nitrosamines are produced when certain foods are cooked, especially at high temperatures. These compounds have been linked to a variety of ailments, from cancer to DNA damage. Though you can often avoid most of these by shunning animal products, carb-rich plant foods cooked with high heat can also form some of these dangerous substances.

- **Fat rancidity:** Certain fats, especially delicate polyunsaturated fats (including essential fatty acids like omega-3s and -6s), are extremely sensitive to heat and can turn into trans fats when cooked. As often as possible, eat your fats in their raw forms to avoid the carcinogenic qualities of heated, rancid fats and oils.

- **Enzymes:** Our bodies produce our own digestive and systemic enzymes, but food contains enzymes too. Food enzymes, which are destroyed by cooking, aid our own digestive enzymes in breaking down nutrients in the stomach. The "enzyme theory" of raw food nutrition is often dismissed, since food enzymes are destroyed anyway once they reach the hydrochloric acid in our stomach, but the fact is that before descending to the acidic lower stomach, the food we eat remains suspended in our upper stomach for about 30 minutes, during which time live food enzymes can indeed aid in nutrient breakdown.

- **Allergies and intolerances:** Raw food is naturally free of most common allergens, such as gluten, wheat, soy, eggs, milk, fish, shellfish, and peanuts. The notable exception to this is tree nuts; raw food has loads of those! As long as you're not nut-sensitive, a high-raw diet can free you from worry regarding most common food allergies and intolerances and the gastrointestinal distress they can cause.

- **Elimination of processed foods:** Although a cooked vegan diet often cuts down one's intake of processed food products, many vegans do still consume an abundance of faux meats and cheeses, white flours and sugars, and over-processed snack foods. Processed food can virtually disappear from your diet if you adopt a high-raw lifestyle.

- **Alkalinity/acidity:** Cooking a food tends to turn its pH more acidic, and while there's a complex scientific explanation behind it, suffice it to say our bodies prefer alkaline-forming foods. The less acidic your diet is, the better your body handles tasks like smoothing digestion and soothing inflammation.

None of this information is meant to scare you into never eating cooked food again. In fact, I don't advocate that at all! Instead, take all of this as evidence that including a variety of raw fruits, vegetables, nuts, and seeds in your daily diet is an excellent way to up your micronutrient intake and absorption and minimize your exposure to allergens and toxins.

ORGANIC FOOD

Organic food tends to be more expensive than conventionally grown food, but the truth is that it's worth the price. Organic produce and other ingredients are grown without the use of pesticides, synthetic fertilizers, genetically modified organisms (GMOs), or ionizing radiation (all potential dangers to our health). Organic farmers tend to emphasize the use of renewable resources and the conservation of soil and water to enhance environmental quality for future generations. On top of all that, organic produce has been found to have higher concentrations of vitamins, minerals, and disease-fighting antioxidants and phytochemicals than conventionally grown produce. And if you ask me, it simply tastes better!

Since organic farming is typically more labor- and cost-intensive, and is not subsidized by the U.S. government, we as consumers must pay a little extra for our organic food. Certain crops are more heavily sprayed with pesticides than others, and are thus more important to buy organic (the "dirty" dozen). On the other hand, another group of vegetables (the "clean" fifteen) retain little to no pesticide residue, so you can feel comfortable saving some dollars there by buying conventional. (See the table on page 14.)

The produce you find at farmers markets may or may not be organic regardless of whether the farm has USDA organic certification; simply ask the farmer about their growing methods or use of pesticides before buying.

Ingredients Guide

Here's a basic run-through of products and ingredients that a raw vegan diet puts to use. I've categorized them in the way that makes the most sense to me, though certain items may belong in multiple categories. For notes on where to find specific products, be sure to check out the Resources section (page 228).

Fruit

It's essential to have a variety of fresh fruit in your house at all times. Fruit makes the perfect snack, and it's the crucial ingredient in most smoothies. Some of my favorites are apples, bananas, berries (strawberries, blueberries, raspberries, blackberries), cherries, grapes, kiwis, mangos, melons (watermelon, honeydew, cantaloupe), peaches, pears, and pineapples. Citrus fruits like limes and (especially) lemons are also great things to have on hand, since their juice is frequently used as an acid in recipes. Only a couple of my recipes include orange juice or oranges, as I'm not a huge fan of the flavor, but I know many people love them!

Good fresh fruit can't be found year-round in many locales, so I keep my freezer stocked with bags of organic frozen fruit, especially in winter. It's particularly convenient for smoothies, since you can throw the frozen fruit right into the blender or food processor.

Dried fruits are also an important staple, especially dates, which are very often used as a sweetener in raw food. Raisins (the dark kind as well as golden raisins), dried cranberries, and dried figs are also great to have.

The "Dirty" Dozen		The "Clean" Fifteen	
Vegetables to buy organic whenever possible, as they tend to be heavily sprayed with chemicals.		Vegetables that tend to retain little or no pesticide residue. Save money by buying conventional.	
apples	potatoes	asparagus	mushrooms
blueberries (domestic)	spinach	avocados	onions
celery	strawberries	cabbage	pineapples
grapes (imported)	sweet bell peppers	cantalope	sweet corn
kale		eggplant	sweet peas
lettuce		grapefruit	sweet potatoes
nectarines (imported)		kiwifruit	watermelon
peaches		mangoes	

Vegetables

Fresh vegetables comprise perhaps the greatest portion of a raw food diet. Some common and delicious veggies include asparagus, broccoli, carrots, cauliflower, celery, corn, mushrooms, onions, peas, and squash (butternut, yellow squash, zucchini). Don't forget about fresh garlic and ginger, which make amazing additions to so many savory recipes. Although avocados, cucumbers, peppers (including bell peppers), and tomatoes are botanically counted among fruits, they are more often considered vegetables in the culinary sense, so I've categorized them here as such. Leafy greens are an important category to include in your diet on a daily basis. The most common are lettuces (such as romaine), cabbage, spinach, and kale, but don't forget about others, such as collard greens, Swiss chard, bok choy, endive, radicchio, arugula, watercress, and more.

Veggies (and fruit, for that matter) tend to be cheaper when they're in season, so I rotate my intake of produce year-round. I'm not big on frozen veggies, with the exception of frozen corn (which is actually a grain rather than a vegetable) and frozen peas, but a couple bags of organic frozen mixed veggies are not a bad thing to have on hand.

Dry-packed sundried tomatoes (technically a fruit) are also often used in raw food, as are common sprouts such as alfalfa or sunflower sprouts.

Nuts

Nuts are a jack-of-all-trades in raw food. They can be chopped, crushed, blended, or eaten whole; they can add texture, flavor, crunch, or creaminess to a dish. Almonds, cashews, macadamia nuts, pecans, and walnuts are the ones I consider essential, and Brazil nuts, hazelnuts, pistachios, and pine nuts are others I like to stock up on. Whenever possible, buy organic raw nuts rather than roasted and/or salted varieties; however, in a pinch, you can use roasted, unsalted varieties. Store raw nuts in your fridge or freezer so their delicate fats don't go rancid. Or, if you want to make your raw nuts shelf-stable, just soak them (referencing the soaking table on page 21) and then dehydrate them for 12 to 24 hours (or bake at 200°F for about 2 hours), until crisp. That way, they'll stay fresh much longer at room temperature.

Nut butters are also a key ingredient in many raw dishes, not to mention one of my favorite snacks ever! I like to keep a jar each of raw almond butter, coconut butter, and cashew butter on hand. Organic raw nut butters can be pricey, so you can use non-raw varieties if you choose. Once opened, store nut butters in the fridge.

Coconuts, though technically a "drupe," not a nut, are another vital ingredient in raw cuisine. Fresh young Thai coconuts are prized for their sweet, electrolyte-rich water and their creamy inner flesh, or "meat." I recommend buying young coconuts at an Asian supermarket, where they are much cheaper. If you're new to fresh coconuts, Google "how to open a young coconut + video" for tutorials on how to open one—it's easy, I swear! In my recipes, I frequently call for a mixture of coconut butter + filtered water to replace young coconut meat if need be, though there's nothing quite like the fresh. If you prefer, you can buy coconut water in aseptic containers. Unsweetened shredded coconut is also handy for many dessert recipes, as well as to make homemade Coconut Butter (recipe on page 92).

FINDING "TRULY RAW" NUTS

Food safety laws in the United States mandate that all raw almonds be pasteurized before sale. This means that even though your almonds may be labeled "raw," chances are they're not. As frustrating as this can be, let's keep it in perspective—it's not the end of the world. When it's all I have access to, I make do with pasteurized almonds. If you can afford it, though, seek out truly raw Italian almonds online (see Resources, page 228) or buy direct from a grower.

For a very different reason, cashews are also not truly raw. The inside of a cashew shell is coated with a resin that is toxic to humans, so the only safe method to open them is by steaming. Nonetheless, cashews play an important role in many raw food recipes, so don't kick them out of your pantry! You can find supposedly "hand-cracked" cashews online for a pretty penny, but whether or not they're truly raw is up for debate.

Seeds

Just as with nuts, seeds are a very versatile ingredient. Flaxseeds, both whole and ground, are often used in the preparation of raw food. They act as a thickener, binder, or crunch-factor. You can make your own flax meal by grinding whole golden flaxseeds in a coffee grinder, but you can also buy pre-ground flaxseed. Chia seeds have a similar gelling effect, but are more shelf-stable. Hempseeds can be costly, but they're so worth it! Sunflower seeds, sesame seeds, and pumpkin seeds (or pepitas) are also oft-used. Sesame seed butter, a.k.a. tahini, is a key ingredient in many recipes. Raw tahini can be expensive and tough to find, so you can always substitute roasted tahini in my recipes. Store all seeds and seed butters in your fridge.

Oils

Unrefined, virgin coconut oil and a high-quality, cold-pressed extra-virgin olive oil are the two most important oils to have in your pantry. A small bottle of sesame oil is nice to have, though I recommend toasted sesame oil instead of raw, as it's far more flavorful. You can also buy nut and seed oils such as flaxseed, hempseed, almond, or macadamia nut, but they must be refrigerated as they are subject to rancidity. I don't use those oils often, though, as I prefer to just eat the whole nut or seed!

Flours and Grains

Almond flour, whether storebought or made at home by drying the leftover pulp from making almond milk, is the flour I use most often in raw recipes. Oat flour and/or buckwheat flour (again, either storebought or made from soaked/dehydrated/ground buckwheat or oat groats) are used frequently as well, often in conjunction with heavier nut flours. Coconut flour absorbs a great deal of water and creates the most tender raw desserts you'll ever eat. Cashew flour makes an appearance now and then, and can easily be made by pulsing raw cashews to a powder in a food processor. (For more details on making your own raw flours, see page 21.) A raw diet typically eschews most grains, but oat groats, pseudograins like quinoa and buckwheat, and wild rice are great for soaking and sprouting. I like to keep raw oat flakes (or simply old-fashioned rolled oats) on hand, too. For all oat products, remember to buy certified gluten-free brands if you're sensitive to the traces of gluten sometimes present on oats.

Sweeteners

Raw agave nectar is the most common all-purpose sweetener used in raw cuisine, despite some recent bad press. When purchasing raw agave, make sure you buy a trusted brand that doesn't cut their product with high-fructose corn syrup. My favorite agave substitute is raw coconut nectar, which is slightly thicker and a touch less sweet, but is a less-processed alternative. (I actually use coconut nectar far more often than agave, but I don't call for it in my recipes primarily because it's more expensive and harder to find.)

Pure maple syrup, though not raw, lends a distinctive flavor to raw recipes and pairs wonderfully with chocolate or cinnamon. Dried dates, especially the Medjool variety, are a fantastic whole-food sweetener. For a powdered sweetener, coconut palm sugar is a low-glycemic granulated sweetener that tastes very much like brown sugar. The best calorie-free sugar substitute is all-natural stevia leaf extract, which can be found in liquid or powdered forms.

There are a plethora of other unrefined sugars out there to check out (some raw and some not); you might explore other options like lucuma powder, yacon syrup, brown rice syrup, Sucanat, molasses, date syrup, date sugar, maple sugar, or evaporated cane juice. (Learn more about agave, stevia, and date syrup in Desserts, pages 196-197.)

Chocolate and Superfoods

Chocolate is a superfood, people! There's nothing like a homemade raw chocolate confection to remind you of the wonders of raw food, so stock your pantry with raw cacao powder (or, alternatively, use carob powder or regular unsweetened cocoa powder), cacao butter, and cacao nibs. Other completely optional superfoods you might keep around are exotic dried fruits like gojiberries, mulberries, and goldenberries; raw protein powders made of hemp and sprouted brown rice; and other nutritious superfood powders like maca, mesquite, spirulina, wheatgrass, or other powdered greens. A bottle of dairy-free probiotic powder, the "good bacteria" that allow you to create tangy, healthful raw yogurts and cheeses (see Resources, page 228, for where to buy), is worth having, and lasts a long time in the refrigerator.

Seasonings

A number of flavoring agents play important roles in raw cuisine. Keep a fully stocked cabinet of dried herbs and spices so you always have a variety of flavor options on hand. Fresh herbs, such as flat-leaf parsley, cilantro, and mint, can really elevate the flavor of a dish. A good-quality sea salt is also essential—don't use the awful bleached, iodized stuff if you can avoid it! Tamari or another soy sauce (like nama shoyu or liquid aminos) comes in very handy, as do vinegars like apple cider, rice, and balsamic. There are many types of miso paste available; I prefer mild white miso, but if you're avoiding soy, seek out chickpea or barley miso. Flavor extracts—at the very least, a good vanilla extract—belong in your kitchen as well. Last but not least, nutritional yeast lends a cheesy, savory taste and a dash of B vitamins to anything you include it in.

Other Important Ingredients

Jarred or bottled olives (I like Kalamata), capers, and chipotle chiles offer big flavor in little packages. I'm not big on sea vegetables generally, but I do keep nori sheets and dulse flakes on hand, and of course kelp noodles, which will keep for months in the fridge. I'm also a fan of Irish moss, a seaweed which can be soaked and blended with water to create a gelatin-like paste, perfect for adding fluffiness to raw "baked" goods. (See page 23 for details on how to make Irish moss gel.)

Fermented foods like kimchi and sauerkraut are popular with raw foodists; you can make your own or buy them. Lecithin, either soy (not raw) or sunflower (raw), will make any blended or puréed item, like nut milks, extra-creamy. If you like sprouts, buy dry beans, lentils, and seeds like alfalfa to grow your own sprouts.

You may choose to include coffee (especially cold-pressed) and tea (especially sun-brewed) in your diet as well. I think certain convenience foods, like good-quality storebought nondairy milks, bottled lemon juice, and nondairy chocolate chips have a place in even a raw food pantry for those "emergency" times when you might need them.

Cutting the Fat

Even though the dietary fats found in raw food are nutritious and health-promoting, some folks may have reasons (such as medical) to reduce their intake of fats from all sources. You can't eliminate too much fat from the recipes in this book, lest the taste or texture suffer, but for those who wish to cut the fat a little bit, I do have some tricks up my sleeve. (Also see Spotlight on Fats, page 187.)

- **Reducing oil:** Anytime a recipe calls for a 1/4 cup or less oil, you can usually get away with reducing it by up to half. If more than 1/4 cup is called for, I'd recommend eliminating no more than 25 percent of the oil.

- **Oats for nuts:** In recipes that make use of ground (but not blended) nuts—such as brownies and blondies, pie and tart crusts, cookies and cakes, energy bars, or even savory seasoned nut meats—you can replace up to one quarter of the nuts in the recipe with an equal amount of raw rolled oat flakes or old-fashioned rolled oats. Be sure to pulse the oats in with the nuts so they're coarsely ground and well-incorporated.

- **More greens, less dressing:** When making any of the kale chip or salad recipes, increase the amount of greens called for without increasing the quantity of dressing or coating. For example, try using 1 1/2 bunches of kale for a batch of chips instead of just one bunch; you'll get more servings out of the batch, and as a result, each serving will be lower in fat and calories.

- **Replacing blended cashews:** You can achieve a similar affect with less fat by using Irish moss. It's a type of seaweed, which, when soaked and blended with water, creates a gelatin-like paste. If you can find it, snatch it up! (It's widely available online, but prices tend to be steep. I find mine very cheap at an Asian superstore; it's labeled *rong bien* in Vietnamese.) Follow the instructions on page 23 to turn the raw Irish moss into a thick gel. Anytime a liberal amount of nuts (at least 3/4 cup, usually cashews) is completely blended into a recipe—particularly in soups, creamy sauces, nut-based hummus, puddings, pie and tart fillings, and ice cream—you can safely replace up to one quarter (or even one third, if you're daring like that) of the cashews with an equal amount of Irish moss gel without adversely affecting the flavor.

- **Bulking up breads:** Irish moss gel has another excellent use: adding volume and an appealing fluffy quality to raw breads. Many of the bread recipes benefit texturally from the addition of Irish moss gel (I've noted each one with a Variation option). As an added bonus, thanks to the extra volume, you'll get more servings from the batch, with each serving being a touch lower in fat.

- **Stretching smoothies:** Once you've mastered the art of Irish moss gel, you might wind up looking for ways to use up the last of a batch. Smoothies are a great way: add about 1/4 cup gel (or even more, if you're not sensitive to the taste) plus an equal amount of filtered water to any smoothie recipe to stretch the number of portions, which will reduce the calories and fat grams per serving.

Equipment Guide

A kitchen full of expensive gadgets is not required to make delicious raw food. Although pricey appliances like dehydrators and high-speed blenders are very useful for churning out gourmet, 100 percent raw delicacies, it's really very easy to get by with just a minimum of equipment. Here's what I use most often in my own kitchen, as well as some alternatives to the more obscure or costly equipment.

Good knives. This one is non-negotiable. At the very least, you should have one sharp, high-quality chef's knife (seven to eight inches in length) and one paring knife (about three inches in length). If you'll be cracking fresh coconuts, you'll also need a heavy cleaver.

Cutting board. Wood, bamboo, plastic, or any other kind you choose—you need a stable (and washable) surface on which to chop your ingredients.

Mandoline. A mandoline will allow you to slice a whole pile of vegetables or fruit paper-thin in record time, but you can always, of course, just do it by hand.

Spiralizer. This optional, inexpensive gadget makes spaghetti-like strands out of zucchini and other vegetables. In lieu of a spiralizer, you can very thinly slice the zucchini lengthwise with a vegetable peeler or mandoline, then carefully cut those slices into fettuccine-shaped pieces. It's quite a bit more work to do it that way, but it gets the job done.

Measuring spoons and cups. You must have a set of measuring spoons as well as both liquid and dry measuring cups.

Mixing bowls, storage containers, and jars. You'll need plenty of vessels in which to make and store your homemade raw goodies, so have a variety of sizes of mixing bowls, storage containers (plastic or, preferably, glass), and Mason jars on hand.

Pans. You can get by with just a baking sheet or two, an 8- or 9-inch square pan, and a 9-inch pie plate, but I'd also recommend a 9-inch tart pan (and/or mini tartlet pans), and a small (6- or 7-inch) springform pan.

Utensils. A vegetable peeler, whisk, sturdy rubber spatula, wooden spoon, box grater, and small strainer are all must-haves. An offset spatula, Microplane grater (for zesting), ring molds, and kitchen scissors are also nice to have.

Strainer/colander. A strainer or colander is good for rinsing off fresh produce or soaked nuts and seeds. If you plan to make nut cheeses like the ones in the chapter Cheeses, Spreads, & Sauces, buy some inexpensive cheesecloth to line your strainer.

Nut milk bag. Crucial for making smooth, homemade nondairy milks, a nylon nut milk bag (or sprouting bag, or paint straining bag) is used to separate the pulp from the milk. See Reources (page 228) for where to get one, and Basic Techniques (page 21) for instructions on how to use one.

Squeeze bottles. You'd be shocked just how useful a couple of inexpensive plastic squeeze bottles can be in your kitchen! You can use them for drizzling sauces, storing condiments, and much more. That said, you can certainly get by without them.

Coffee/spice grinder. A coffee grinder or spice grinder is wonderful for making fresh flax meal and spice powders, but it isn't a necessity.

Food processor. A food processor is essential for a good deal of raw food preparation. You may be able to get around it sometimes by chopping ingredients by hand, but more often than not, a food processor is indispensable. It doesn't have to be fancy—you can easily find a good one for under $100—and all you need is the standard S-blade that comes with it. I have both an 11-cup model and a 3-cup mini version, but all you really need is the larger, standard size.

Ice cream maker. Another optional item, ice cream makers are a fun and easy way to churn up raw vegan frozen treats. However, I would never deem it a kitchen necessity.

High-speed blender. Just a few years ago, I would've found the idea of a $600 blender ludicrous. Now, I wouldn't give mine up for anything! A super-powerful blender such as a Vitamix or Blendtec will transform the way you look at smoothies, soups, sauces, and much more. It's definitely an investment, but it'll last a lifetime, and you won't believe the dreamily smooth purées it'll turn out.

I realize, however, that a $400 to $600 appliance is not within many people's budget, so don't fret if all you have is a more modest blender. Your purées may be slightly less smooth, but it'll still do the trick. When blending nuts and seeds, you may just want to soak them an extra couple hours if using a regular blender.

Dehydrator. Dehydration is the process of evaporating liquid out of foods. In raw cuisine, a dehydrator is used to "bake" foods at temperatures below 118°F (48°C) in order to preserve all the nutrients, vitamins, and enzymes within. Dehydrators are incredibly versatile—you can make just-moist-enough cakes, shatteringly crisp crackers, perfectly chewy burgers or cookies, and much more, all without damaging a single nutrient. Excalibur, TSM, and Sedona are all top-quality brands. For each dehydrator tray, you'll also need a Teflex sheet, a nonstick surface to place wet foods on until they're dry enough to transfer to mesh trays. Any time a recipe directs you to dehydrate, set the temperature of your machine anywhere between 105°F and 115°F (40 to 46°C).

Not everyone wants to invest in a dehydrator, at least not right away, so for those just getting started in raw food, I've provided conventional oven-baking directions for almost every recipe in this book. While it's true that if you use a regular oven, your food won't be technically raw (i.e., it will be cooked above 118°F), your finished product will still be composed of all-natural, ultra-healthful fruits, vegetables, nuts, and seeds. In fact, you may enjoy the results so much that you decide you want to add a dehydrator to your kitchen.

Alternatively, you can mimic dehydration by using your oven on its lowest ("warm") setting and leaving the door cracked, although this method does waste a lot of energy.

Other appliances, such as juicers, stand mixers, and immersion blenders, can also be great additions to any kitchen, but aren't required for any of the recipes in this book.

Basic Techniques & Guidelines

Soaking Nuts and Seeds

In raw food prep, nuts and seeds are soaked for multiple reasons. Some, particularly nuts with skins such as almonds, walnuts, and pecans, contain enzyme inhibitors that must be neutralized through soaking so that our bodies can more comfortably digest them. Other times, nuts and seeds are soaked for texture's sake, to allow them to soften and become easier to blend. When a recipe calls for "1 cup nuts, soaked," simply place one cup of dry nuts in a bowl, cover with cold filtered water, and let sit at room temperature for the amount of time indicated in the table below. In a recipe where the nuts or seeds require soaking, the amount called for is always measured dry, before the soaking step. The soaking time need not be precise; if you only have 30 minutes to soak some cashews, for instance, just use warm water instead of cold, and place the bowl in a warm dehydrator to speed the soaking process.

Nuts and Seeds: To Soak or Not to Soak?

Nut/Seed	Soaking Time	Nut/Seed	Soaking Time
Almonds	8 to 12 hours	Pecans	4 to 6 hours
Brazilnuts	6 to 8 hours	Pine nuts	1 to 2 hours
Cashews	2 to 4 hours	Pistachios	2 to 4 hours
Flaxseeds	do not soak	Pumpkin seeds	2 to 4 hours
Hazelnuts	6 to 8 hours	Sesame Seeds	do not soak
Hempseeds	do not soak	Sunflower seeds	2 to 4 hours
Macadamia nuts	2 to 4 hours	Walnuts	6 to 8 hours

You may also choose to soak and dehydrate all your nuts to extend their shelf life. In that case, soak the nuts for the proper amount of time, then transfer to mesh-lined dehydrator trays and dehydrate for 24 to 48 hours (or bake at 200°F for about 2 hours), until crisp.

When a recipe calls for "1 cup dry nuts," do not soak before preparing the recipe.

Straining Nut Milks

Hold a nut milk bag open over a large bowl or pitcher and simply pour your freshly-blended nut milks into the bag. Twist, squeeze, and knead the bag (with clean hands!) to extract all the milk (taking care not to spill it outside the bowl) from the pulp, which can then be dehydrated or baked to make flour.

Making Flours

- **Almond Flour.** To make almond flour, strain freshly made Almond Milk (page 30) through a nut milk bag, reserving the pulp. Transfer the pulp to a Teflex-lined de-hydrator tray and dehydrate for 8 to 12 hours or overnight, until dry. Alternatively, transfer the pulp to a parchment paper-lined baking sheet and bake at 200°F for 1 to 2 hours, or until dry. Crumble and store in the refrigerator or freezer.

- **Oat Flour.** To make oat flour, soak whole raw oat groats in cold filtered water for 8 to 12 hours or overnight. After rinsing and draining, transfer the oats to a mesh-lined dehydrator tray and dehydrate for 24 hours, or until dry. Alternatively, transfer the oats to a parchment paper-lined baking sheet and bake at 200°F for 2 to 4 hours, or until dry. Transfer the dried oats to a high-speed blender or food processor and process into a flour-like consistency. Sift the flour to remove any large, hard crumbs. Store in the refrigerator.

  For an even easier way to make oat flour, place raw rolled oat flakes or old-fashioned rolled oats in a food processor and pulse until finely ground.

- **Buckwheat Flour.** To make buckwheat flour, soak whole raw buckwheat groats in cold filtered water for 15 to 30 minutes (no longer!). After rinsing and draining, transfer the buckwheat to a mesh-lined dehydrator tray and dehydrate for 12 to 24 hours, or until dry. Alternatively, transfer the buckwheat to a parchment paper-lined baking sheet and bake at 200°F for 2 to 3 hours, or until dry. Transfer the dried buckwheat to a high-speed blender or food processor and process into a flour-like consistency. Sift the flour to remove any large, hard crumbs. Store in the refrigerator.

- **Cashew Flour.** To make cashew flour, place raw cashews in the bowl of a food processor and pulse until very finely ground. Store in the refrigerator.

Melting Oils and Butters

Coconut oil and cacao butter both need to be melted before being put to use in any recipe, unless otherwise specified. The amounts of coconut oil and cacao butter I call for in recipes are always measured after melting.

- **Coconut Oil and Butter.** To melt coconut oil, you can place the whole jar in a warm dehydrator for 10 to 20 minutes, or until melted, or set it in a bowl of hot water (making sure it stands upright). If you only need a small amount, melt a couple spoonfuls in a double boiler over very low heat, stirring constantly, or in a small bowl placed carefully in a larger bowl of hot water (making sure no water gets into the smaller bowl). Unused melted coconut oil can simply be poured back into the original jar.

  Coconut butter can also be softened before using; it's not always necessary, but it makes it easier to mix and measure. To do so, place the whole jar in a warm dehydrator for 15 to 30 minutes, or until softened, or set it in a bowl of hot water (making sure it stands upright). If you only need a small amount, melt a few spoonfuls in a double boiler over very low heat, stirring often, or in a small bowl placed carefully in a larger bowl of hot water (making sure no water gets into the smaller bowl). Unused softened coconut butter can simply be transferred back into the original jar.

- **Cacao Butter.** To melt cacao butter, chop it roughly with a sharp knife, transfer it to a bowl, and place it in a warm dehydrator for 20 to 30 minutes, or until melted, stirring occasionally. Alternatively, you can melt cacao butter in a double boiler over very low heat, stirring constantly, or place it in a jar and set it in a bowl of hot water (making sure it stands upright). Unused melted cacao butter can be chilled until solid, then transferred in a chunk back to its original container.

Freezing Bananas

I keep a stash of peeled, frozen bananas in my freezer at all times. Let your bananas get as ripe as possible (with plenty of dark brown spots on the skin) before peeling and arranging them on a baking sheet. Freeze them for at least 8 hours or overnight and then transfer them to a plastic zip-top bag to store in the freezer. The more ripe your bananas are when you freeze them, the more natural sweetness they'll lend to your recipes.

Making Irish Moss Gel

If you are able to acquire Irish moss (see Resources, page 228), it is a type of seaweed with multiple uses in raw food preparation. You'll find it makes an excellent addition to raw breads and pastries, making them lighter, fluffier, and almost baked-tasting. Before using it, you must turn the Irish moss into a gel to make it easier to pulse or blend into things. (See Cutting the Fat on page 18.)

To make Irish moss gel, place 1 cup packed Irish moss in a large bowl and cover with 3 to 4 cups cold filtered water. Soak for 3 to 4 hours, then rinse and drain well. Combine the soaked Irish moss and 1/2 cup cold filtered water in a high-speed blender and blend until smooth (you'll probably need to use the tamper for this). Add additional water, 1 to 2 tablespoons at a time, as needed to blend, only adding the bare minimum amount necessary to make a smooth purée. Use right away or transfer the mixture to a small container and refrigerate for up to a week.

The Raw Vegan Pantry

Here is a comprehensive list of ingredients for a raw vegan pantry. Remember, you certainly don't need to have everything on this list to begin experimenting with raw food. Take inventory of your fridge and pantry, then flip though this book, keeping an eye out for ingredients you have. You're sure to find numerous things you can whip up, especially if you take note of the substitution options offered at the end of every recipe.

Fruit

Fresh:

Apples
Bananas
Berries (assorted)
Cherries
Citrus fruits (lemons, limes, oranges)
Grapes
Kiwis
Mangos
Melons (assorted)
Peaches
Pears
Pineapple

Frozen:

Berries (assorted)
Cherries
Mangos
Peaches
Pineapple

Dried:

Dates
Raisins
Cranberries
Figs
Apricots

Vegetables

Fresh:

Asparagus
Avocados
Bell peppers
Broccoli
Carrots
Cauliflower
Celery
Corn
Cucumbers
Garlic
Ginger
Leafy greens (assorted)
Mushrooms
Onions
Sprouts
Squash (summer and winter)
Tomatoes (fresh and sundried)

Frozen:

Corn
Peas

Nuts

Almonds
Cashews
Macadamia nuts
Pecans
Walnuts
Brazil nuts
Hazelnuts
Pine nuts
Pistachios
Coconuts: fresh young Thai coconuts, unsweetened shredded coconut, coconut water

Seeds

Ground flaxseed (flax meal)
Chia seeds
Sesame seeds
Hempseeds
Sunflower seeds
Whole golden flaxseed
Pumpkin seeds

Nut and Seed Butters

Almond butter
Coconut butter
Cashew butter
Tahini (sesame seed butter)

Oils
Unrefined virgin coconut oil
Extra-virgin olive oil
Toasted sesame oil
Nut oils (assorted)
Seed oils (flax, hemp)

Flours and Grains
Almond flour
Buckwheat flour
Oat flour
Coconut flour
Cashew flour
Wild rice
Buckwheat groats
Oat groats
Raw oat flakes, old-fashioned rolled oats

Sweeteners
Raw agave nectar or coconut nectar
Dried dates (Medjool and/or deglet noor)
Pure maple syrup (grade B)
Coconut palm sugar
Stevia (liquid and/or powder)

Herbs and Spices
Dried:
Basil
Black pepper
Cardamom
Cayenne pepper
Chili powder
Cinnamon
Coriander
Crushed red pepper flakes
Cumin (ground)
Cumin seeds
Curry powder
Fennel seeds
Garlic powder
Onion powder
Oregano
Paprika
Pumpkin pie spice
Rosemary
Saffron (optional)
Sage
Sea salt
Thyme
Turmeric

Fresh:
Flat-leaf parsley
Cilantro
Mint

Seasonings
Miso paste (preferably white)
Nutritional yeast
Tamari soy sauce, nama shoyu, or liquid aminos
Real vanilla extract
Other flavor extracts (almond, coffee, etc.)
Vinegars (assorted)

Chocolate & Optional Superfoods
Raw cacao powder, carob powder, or un-
sweetened cocoa powder
Cacao butter
Cacao nibs
Gojiberries, mulberries, and/or goldenberries
Hemp or sprouted brown rice protein powder
Maca powder
Mesquite powder
Powdered greens supplement
Spirulina powder
Wheatgrass juice powder
Dairy-free probiotic powder

Other
Sea vegetables: nori, dulse flakes, kelp
noodles, Irish moss
Lecithin (soy or sunflower)
Jarred olives, capers, and chipotle chiles
Dried beans and lentils (for sprouting)
Coffee and/or tea
Good-quality storebought nondairy milks,
bottled lemon juice, nondairy chocolate
chips, and other convenience foods

General Recipe Guidelines

Ingredient Basics for All Recipes

There are some basic facts about the recipe ingredients that hold true for all the recipes, unless otherwise specified. Keep these general points in mind as you prepare the recipes:

- All ingredients used are raw and organic. If raw or organic items are not available to you, however, you can substitute a non-raw, conventional alternative.

- All oils are cold-pressed and virgin, with the exception of sesame oil.

- Dehydration is conducted between 105 and 115°F (40 to 46°C).

- All produce is thoroughly washed before use.

- Soaked nuts, seeds, sundried tomatoes, and dates should be rinsed and drained thoroughly before proceeding with the recipe.

Advance Prep

Several of the recipes require some advance prep before the dish can be made. Keep this in mind when deciding to make a recipe so you're sure to have the various components ready when you are. This will help streamline the recipe prep and maximize your time in the kitchen. Please note that I do not mention prep for certain staples you've presumably already made or bought and have on hand (such as almond milk or various flours), and I don't include little things that can be done just a few minutes before beginning a recipe (like chopping veggies or melting coconut oil). I do, however, note when you should perform tasks such as soaking nuts or seeds or preparing component recipes in advance.

Remember that if you don't have time or forgot to prep in advance, those steps can sometimes be bypassed by utilizing some of the substitutions listed at the bottom of a recipe.

Substitutions and Personal Preferences

Just as one man's trash is another man's treasure, one person's least-favorite food can be another's most-loved. Though some things are universal when it comes to human tastes—sweet, salty, sour, bitter, umami, etc.—beyond that, it's every one for himself. To the best of my ability, I've crafted these recipes to be delectable to all palates, but each individual possesses a unique set of taste buds. Besides the considerations of budget and availability, this is another reason I've provided so many substitution options for every recipe. Each recipe, as written, is what I consider its most delicious incarnation. However, you shouldn't hesitate to try the substitution suggestions provided to tailor the dish to your own liking. Though I can't vouch for every permutation of these numerous substitution possibilities, I have tested (and approved) a great number of them. Similarly, if you are sensitive to salt or sugar, feel free to reduce the amounts of sea salt, sweeteners, or anything else in the recipes. You're in charge here! I fully encourage you to play around and experiment with these recipes, molding them to your and your family's own tastes and preferences. I hope you love the results!

Recipes Are Gluten-Free and Soy-Free

The recipes in *Practically Raw* are gluten-free as well as soy-free. In recipes that call for oats, tamari, or miso, readers are reminded to use gluten-free oats and tamari and soy-free miso.

About the Icons

LF = Lower-Fat

Recipes designated as LF generally contain less than 25 to 30 percent of calories from fat. In some cases, when a recipe yields fewer than 10 total fat grams per serving, I have marked it as lower-fat as long as no more than 40 percent of its calories come from fat. This allows me to include items that are low in both calories and total fat, even if the percentage of fat calories slightly exceeds 30 percent.

CO = Cooked Option

Recipes with the CO icon include directions for how to cook or bake the dish using a conventional oven or stovetop range instead of a dehydrator, if desired.

‹30 = 30 Minutes or Less

Recipes marked <30 require no more than 30 minutes of hands-on time to make (not including chilling time or passive prep work like soaking nuts). I've chosen to exclude any and all recipes requiring dehydration or baking, even if the prep time is less than 30 minutes, as well as any that require component recipes to be prepared in advance.

Milks & Smoothies

Raw nut and seed milks are two of the simplest and most healthful beverages you can make. They have the same creaminess and versatility of soy or dairy milk, but with better flavor and more unadulterated, intact nutrients. These nondairy milks show up frequently in my recipes, so it's great to have a batch on hand at all times; they will keep for at least three days in the fridge.

Smoothies are a staple in my diet. How else can one manage to fit two to three servings of fruit and a huge handful of leafy greens into one travel-friendly breakfast or snack? The possibilities for smoothies are endless, so feel free to use mine as a springboard to create your own. I use a high-speed blender, but most regular blenders will work just fine. Since smoothies should be consumed immediately after they're made to ensure the best taste and texture (and to prevent nutrient loss through oxidation), these recipes have fairly small yields, but you can double or even triple any of them if you're feeding the whole family.

Purple Pearberry Smoothie, page 37.

Almond Milk

YIELD: ABOUT 5 CUPS `LF` `‹30`

Almond milk is the king of all-purpose nondairy milks—mild in flavor, low in calories, and a cinch to make at home. If you'll be using the milk in a savory recipe, omit the dates.

1 cup almonds, soaked for 8 to 12 hours and drained
5 cups filtered water
3 pitted dates (optional)
1/2 teaspoon lemon juice
Pinch of sea salt

Combine all ingredients in a high-speed blender and blend until smooth. Strain the mixture through a nut milk bag (see page 21 for instructions) and chill thoroughly.

Per cup*: about 70 calories, 2.5g fat (trace sat), 10g carbs, 1g fiber, 2g protein

*These nutritional values are approximate, due to variations in milk yield of almonds.

SUBSTITUTIONS

- Almonds: hazelnuts, Brazil nuts, or almost any other type of nut you like
- Dates: 1 to 2 tablespoons agave nectar, coconut nectar, any other liquid sweetener, or stevia to taste

VARIATIONS

- Vanilla Almond Milk: Blend in 1 teaspoon vanilla extract.
- Almond Cream: Reduce the water to 2 to 3 cups to make a rich cream.
- Extra-creamy milk: Blend in 1 teaspoon sunflower lecithin.
- Chocolate Almond Milk: Blend in cacao powder or nibs and additional date(s) to taste.

TIP

Save the leftover pulp to make almond flour (see page 21-22).

Coconut Milk

YIELD: ABOUT 1 1/2 CUPS   `‹30`

When you want to add richness to a recipe, look no further than fresh coconut milk. It's thinner and much lower in fat than the canned stuff, but it still tastes plenty creamy.

1/2 cup chopped young coconut meat

1 cup coconut water

1/2 teaspoon lemon juice

Pinch of sea salt

Combine all ingredients in a high-speed blender and blend until smooth. Strain the mixture through a nut milk bag, if desired, and chill thoroughly before serving.

Per 1/2 cup: 62 calories, 4.6g fat (4g sat), 5g carbs, 2g fiber, 1g protein

SUBSTITUTION

Coconut meat: 1/4 cup unsweetened shredded coconut (making sure to strain the mixture through a nut milk bag after blending)

PREPARING YOUNG COCONUT MEAT

If you've never hacked and scraped a young Thai coconut (the large white kind with a conical top, not the fuzzy brown variety) before, please Google "how to open a young coconut + video" and watch a couple of tutorials online before attempting to open one yourself. It's very important to see how it's done, rather than just read instructions! Once you're confident in your hacking skills, you can save time and money by purchasing a case of nine coconuts (try your local Asian market for the best prices) and harvesting the water and meat all at once. Fresh coconut water will keep in the fridge for 1 to 2 days, and young coconut meat will last for 3 to 4 days when refrigerated. For longer-term storage, coconut water and meat can be frozen separately for up to one month; simply defrost fully before using in any recipe. I like to freeze chopped coconut meat and coconut water in 1/4 or 1/2 cup portions so that when I want to use some in a recipe, I can easily thaw a premeasured amount.

Hempseed Milk

YIELD: ABOUT 2 CUPS

If you like your nondairy milk to have plenty of protein and omega-3 fats, then hempseed milk is for you. And the best part? It doesn't have to be strained! Just stir or shake well before serving.

- 1/4 cup hempseeds
- 2 cups filtered water
- 2 teaspoons agave nectar
- 1/2 teaspoon lemon juice
- Pinch of sea salt

Combine all ingredients in a high-speed blender and blend until smooth. (You can blend in an additional 1 to 2 tablespoons of hempseeds if you want a thicker, richer milk.) Chill thoroughly before serving.

Per cup: 136 calories, 9g fat (1g sat), 6.8g carbs, 1g fiber, 7.3g protein

SUBSTITUTIONS

Agave nectar: coconut nectar, any other liquid sweetener, 1 pitted date, or stevia to taste

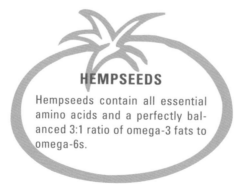

HEMPSEEDS

Hempseeds contain all essential amino acids and a perfectly balanced 3:1 ratio of omega-3 fats to omega-6s.

Maple Cinnamon Pecan Milk

YIELD: ABOUT 3 CUPS `‹30`

One word to describe this milk: luxurious. It's like pecan pie in a glass. I actually prefer it un-strained; it tastes thicker and richer that way.

1/2 cup raw pecans, soaked for 4 to 6 hours and drained
2 cups filtered water
2 tablespoons maple syrup
1/2 teaspoon vanilla extract
1/2 teaspoon lemon juice
1/4 teaspoon ground cinnamon
Pinch of sea salt

Combine all ingredients in a high-speed blender and blend until smooth. Strain the mixture through a nut milk bag, if desired, and chill thoroughly before serving.

Per cup: 162 calories, 13g fat (1g sat), 11.8g carbs, 2g fiber, 1.7g protein

SUBSTITUTIONS

Maple syrup: agave nectar, coconut nectar, any other liquid sweetener, 3 to 4 pitted dates, or stevia to taste

Basic Green Smoothie

YIELD: ABOUT 2 CUPS `LF` `‹30`

For a straight-up dose of leafy green goodness, you need nothing more than a couple frozen bananas and some nondairy milk. Sometimes, it's nice to go back to basics. (See photo, page 39.)

2 frozen ripe bananas, broken into chunks
1 cup Almond Milk (page 30)
1 cup packed fresh spinach
2 pitted dates (optional)

Combine all ingredients in a high-speed blender and blend until very smooth. Add a few ice cubes and blend again if a colder smoothie or thicker texture is desired. Serve immediately.

Per cup: 164 calories, 1.9g fat (trace sat), 37.7g carbs, 5g fiber, 2.8g protein

SUBSTITUTIONS

- Almond Milk: any other nondairy milk
- Spinach: 1 to 2 large kale leaves, tough stems removed
- Dates: 1 tablespoon agave nectar, coconut nectar, any other liquid sweetener, or stevia to taste

A NOTE ON GREENS AND DATES

Although only two of my smoothie recipes contain spinach or kale, I actually include greens in all the smoothies I make at home. I encourage you to add greens to your smoothies, too, whenever possible—it will muddy the color a little bit, but it will send the nutritional value through the roof.

Please note that I do include the optional ingredients such as dates and hemp protein when calculating the nutrition info for my smoothies.

Berries Over Greens Smoothie

YIELD: ABOUT 3 CUPS **LF** **‹30**

If you're just getting into green smoothies, then berries, especially a mixture of them, are your best friends. They cover up any hint of leafiness in a smoothie like this.

1 frozen ripe banana, broken into chunks
1 cup Almond Milk (page 30)
1/2 cup fresh or frozen raspberries
1/2 cup fresh or frozen blackberries
1/2 cup fresh or frozen blueberries
1 cup packed fresh spinach
1 to 2 pitted dates (optional)

Combine all ingredients in a high-speed blender and blend until very smooth. Add a few ice cubes and blend again if a colder smoothie or thicker texture is desired. Serve immediately.

Per cup: 101 calories, 1.3g fat (trace sat), 22.6g carbs, 6g fiber, 2g protein

SUBSTITUTIONS

- Almond Milk: any other nondairy milk
- Berries: any combination of berries totaling 1 1/2 cups
- Spinach: 2 to 3 large kale leaves, tough stems removed
- Dates: 1 tablespoon agave nectar, coconut nectar, any other liquid sweetener, or stevia to taste

SUPERFOOD SMOOTHIE INFUSION

Yield: about 2 cups   `LF` `<30`

I like to keep a premixed container of this superfood-packed mixture in my fridge at all times. Add a spoonful or two to any smoothie recipe for a boost of fiber, protein, and omega-3 fats. If you're missing any of the ingredients (or if there's one you dislike), no biggie—just leave it out.

3/4 cup ground flaxseed

1/2 cup hemp protein powder

1/4 cup chia seeds

1/4 cup maca powder

1/4 cup spirulina

2 tablespoons dulse flakes

Combine all ingredients in a small container with a lid. Close the lid and shake the container to mix. Blend 2 tablespoons into any smoothie recipe to instantly boost the nutrition. Store the mixture in the refrigerator.

Per serving: 64 calories, 3.1g fat (trace sat), 5.4g carbs, 3g fiber, 4.5g protein

Tropic Thunder Smoothie

YIELD: ABOUT 3 CUPS

Get ready for an island delight! Pineapple is the #1 source for the inflammation-quelling enzyme bromelain, so this smoothie will calm your body and your mood. Many people dislike the gritty, somewhat grassy texture and taste of hemp protein at first. I didn't fall in love with it until I tried it paired with pineapple, like in this piña-colada-esque sipper.

1 frozen ripe banana, broken into chunks

1 1/2 cups coconut water

3/4 cup chopped pineapple, fresh or frozen

1/2 medium ripe mango, peeled, seeded, and chopped (or 1/2 cup frozen mango chunks)

2 to 4 tablespoons hemp protein powder (optional)

1/4 cup chopped young coconut meat (optional)

1 to 2 pitted dates (optional)

Combine all ingredients in a high-speed blender and blend until very smooth. Add a few ice cubes and blend again if a colder smoothie or thicker texture is desired. Serve immediately.

Per cup: 145 calories, 3.2g fat (2g sat), 27.9g carbs, 5g fiber, 4.2g protein

SUBSTITUTIONS

- Coconut water: orange juice, almond milk, any other nondairy milk, or filtered water
- Hemp protein: any other vegan protein powder
- Coconut meat: 1 to 2 tablespoons Coconut Butter (page 92)
- Dates: 1 tablespoon agave nectar, coconut nectar, any other liquid sweetener, or stevia to taste

Purple Pearberry Smoothie

YIELD: ABOUT 3 CUPS `LF` `‹30`

When I randomly happened upon the combo of blackberries and pear one day, I was hooked. Both fruits contain impressive amounts of fiber, so this smoothie is great for digestion. Hemp protein pairs especially nicely with pear, too, so add it here if you like. (See photo, page 28.)

1 frozen ripe banana, broken into chunks

3/4 cup Almond Milk (page 30)

1 large ripe pear, peeled if desired, cored, and chopped

1 cup fresh or frozen blackberries

2 tablespoons hemp protein powder (optional)

2 pitted dates (optional)

Combine all ingredients in a high-speed blender and blend until very smooth. Add a few ice cubes and blend again if a colder smoothie or thicker texture is desired. Serve immediately.

Per cup: 140 calories, 1.6g fat (trace sat), 30.9g carbs, 7g fiber, 4g protein

SUBSTITUTIONS

- Almond Milk: any other nondairy milk
- Hemp protein: any other vegan protein powder
- Dates: 1 tablespoon agave nectar, coconut nectar, any other liquid sweetener, or stevia to taste

---

FREEZING BANANAS

It's advisable to keep a supply of frozen bananas in your freezer at all times. Allow the bananas to ripen (with plenty of dark brown spots on the skin), then peel them. Arrange them on a baking sheet and freeze them for at least 8 hours or overnight. Once frozen, transfer them to a plastic zip-top bag to store in the freezer. The more ripe the bananas when you freeze them, the more natural sweetness they'll lend to your recipes.

Cherry Mash Smoothie

YIELD: ABOUT 2 1/2 CUPS   `‹30`

Ever had one of those delicious, terrible-for-you Cherry Mash candies? This is like one of those, but made with real food, and served in a frosty glass. Cherries contain anthocyanins that have been found to reduce inflammation and other risk factors for heart disease.

1 frozen ripe banana, broken into chunks
1 1/4 cups Almond Milk (page 30)
1 cup pitted fresh or frozen cherries
2 tablespoons Coconut Butter (page 92)
2 pitted dates (optional)

Combine all ingredients in a high-speed blender and blend until very smooth. Add a few ice cubes and blend again if a colder smoothie or thicker texture is desired. Serve immediately.

Per cup: 192 calories, 8.9g fat (7g sat), 28.6g carbs, 5g fiber, 3g protein

SUBSTITUTIONS

- Almond Milk: any other nondairy milk
- Coconut Butter: 1/4 cup chopped young coconut meat
- Dates: 1 tablespoon agave nectar, coconut nectar, any other liquid sweetener, or stevia to taste

Peaches 'n Creamsicle Smoothie (below), Cherry Mash Smoothie (page 38), Basic Green Smoothie (page 33)

Peaches 'n Creamsicle Smoothie

YIELD: ABOUT 3 CUPS   **LF** **‹30**

Since I'm not a fan of strong orange flavor, I take this creamsicle-like smoothie down a different path by using peaches. Mango or papaya would work just as well. Coconut butter adds extra unctuousness, but isn't essential.

    1 frozen ripe banana, broken into chunks
    1 cup Almond Milk (page 30)
    1/2 cup orange juice
    1 cup fresh or frozen sliced peaches
    1 tablespoon Coconut Butter (page 92) (optional)
    2 pitted dates (optional)

Combine all ingredients in a high-speed blender and blend until very smooth. Add a few ice cubes and blend again if a colder smoothie or thicker texture is desired. Serve immediately.

SUBSTITUTIONS

- Almond Milk: any other nondairy milk
- Orange juice: coconut water or filtered water
- Peaches: mango or papaya
- Dates: 1 tablespoon agave nectar, coconut nectar, any other liquid sweetener, or stevia to taste

Mango Lassi

YIELD: ABOUT 3 CUPS   `LF` `‹30`

Indian restaurants often serve refreshing mango lassis to cool your palate after a spicy curry. As such, this goes especially well with Vegetable Korma Masala (page 158). Include a pinch of ground cardamom for extra Indian flair.

2 large ripe mangos, peeled, seeded, and chopped (or 2 cups frozen mango chunks)

1/2 cup coconut water

1/2 cup chopped young coconut meat

1/2 teaspoon lemon juice

Pinch of sea salt

Combine all ingredients in a high-speed blender and blend until very smooth. (If using frozen mango, you can add 1/4 to 1/2 cup filtered water or additional coconut water if the mixture is too thick.) Add a few ice cubes and blend again if a colder drink or thicker texture is desired. Serve immediately.

Per cup: 145 calories, 4.9g fat (4g sat), 27g carbs, 4g fiber, 1.2g protein

SUBSTITUTIONS

- Coconut water: filtered water plus 1 tablespoon agave nectar or other liquid sweetener
- Coconut meat: 1/4 cup Coconut Butter (page 92) plus 1/4 cup filtered water

Hemp Horchata

YIELD: ABOUT 2 CUPS `‹30`

Inspired by my most-loved elixir at one of my favorite restaurants, Bliss Raw Café in Dallas, Texas, this sweet 'n cinnamon-y treat can double as a drinkable dessert.

1/2 cup hempseeds
1 1/2 cups filtered water
2 tablespoons agave nectar
2 to 3 teaspoons ground cinnamon
2 to 3 teaspoons mesquite powder (optional)
1/2 teaspoon lemon juice
Pinch of sea salt
2 tablespoons melted coconut oil

Combine all ingredients except the coconut oil in a high-speed blender and blend until very smooth. With the machine running, pour in the coconut oil in a thin stream, blending until well-incorporated. Refrigerate until thoroughly chilled, shake well, and then serve.

Per 1/2 cup serving: 209 calories, 15.8g fat (7g sat), 10.8g carbs, 2g fiber, 7.4g protein

SUBSTITUTIONS

- Agave nectar: coconut nectar, any other liquid sweetener, or stevia to taste
- Mesquite powder: maca powder
- Filtered water: coconut water

POD POWDER

Naturally sweet mesquite pod powder helps balance blood sugar and provides healthy doses of dietary fiber, protein, and minerals.

Chocolate-Covered Strawberry Smoothie

YIELD: ABOUT 3 CUPS ▪ LF ▪ ‹30

Strawberries, often underappreciated in the nutrition department, are one of the lowest-calorie fruits and are a good source of fiber and vitamin C. Although you can use fresh strawberries, frozen ones work better, as they help give the smoothie a thicker, icier texture. I recommend including the dates here to help take the bitter edge off the cacao nibs.

1 frozen ripe banana, broken into chunks
2 cups Almond Milk (page 30)
1 1/2 cups frozen strawberries
2 heaping tablespoons cacao nibs
1 teaspoon vanilla extract
2 pitted dates (optional)

Combine all ingredients in a high-speed blender and blend until very smooth. Add a few ice cubes and blend again if a colder smoothie or thicker texture is desired. Serve immediately.

Per cup: 130 calories, 4.5g fat (2g sat), 22.9g carbs, 5g fiber, 2.8g protein

SUBSTITUTIONS

- Almond Milk: any other nondairy milk
- Frozen strawberries: frozen raspberries, or fresh strawberries or raspberries (decreasing the amount of almond milk to 1 1/2 cups)
- Cacao nibs: 2 tablespoons raw cacao powder, unsweetened cocoa powder, or carob powder plus 1 extra pitted date
- Dates: 1 tablespoon agave nectar, coconut nectar, any other liquid sweetener, or stevia to taste

Apple Pie Smoothie

YIELD: ABOUT 2 CUPS   **LF**   **‹30**

I've made this as a bedtime snack just as often as I've made it for breakfast. You'll feel like you're eating a big, chilled slice of homemade apple pie—just without all the chewing!

1 large apple, peeled if desired, cored, and chopped
3/4 cup Almond Milk (page 30)
6 to 8 walnut halves, dry or soaked and drained
3 pitted dates
1/2 teaspoon ground cinnamon
1/2 teaspoon vanilla extract
Pinch of sea salt

Combine all ingredients in a high-speed blender and blend until very smooth. Add a few ice cubes and blend again if a colder smoothie or thicker texture is desired. Serve immediately.

Per cup: 147 calories, 5.1g fat (trace sat), 25.3g carbs, 4g fiber, 2.1g protein

SUBSTITUTIONS

- Almond Milk: apple juice or any other nondairy milk
- Walnuts: pecans
- Dates: 1 tablespoon maple syrup, agave nectar, coconut nectar, any other liquid sweetener, or stevia to taste

VARIATIONS

- Include 2 to 4 tablespoons soaked and drained raw cashews for an extra-rich and creamy version.
- Sprinkle each serving of the finished smoothie with 1/8 teaspoon freshly grated nutmeg.
- Include a handful of spinach to make it a Green Apple Pie Smoothie.

Cocoa Corruption Smoothie

YIELD: ABOUT 2 1/2 CUPS   `‹30›`

You knew I had to include at least one naughty chocolate smoothie, didn't you?! This indulgent cacao-laced treat is a surprisingly good source of both fiber and protein.

2 frozen ripe bananas, broken into chunks

1 1/4 cups Almond Milk (page 30)

1/4 cup cacao nibs

2 tablespoons Almond Butter (page 92)

1 teaspoon vanilla extract

2 pitted dates (optional)

Combine all ingredients in a high-speed blender and blend until very smooth. Add a few ice cubes and blend again if a colder smoothie or thicker texture is desired. Serve immediately.

Per cup: 275 calories, 15g fat (4g sat), 36.3g carbs, 8g fiber, 6g protein

SUBSTITUTIONS

- Almond Milk: any other nondairy milk
- Cacao nibs: 3 tablespoons raw cacao powder, unsweetened cocoa powder, or carob powder plus 1 extra pitted date
- Almond Butter: cashew butter or peanut butter
- Dates: 1 tablespoon agave nectar, coconut nectar, any other liquid sweetener, or stevia to taste

VARIATIONS

- Add 1 to 3 teaspoons of maca powder.
- After blending all ingredients together, with the machine still running, stream in 1 tablespoon of melted coconut oil.

﹏ Breakfast & Brunch

Because I'm a sweets-for-breakfast kind of girl, you'll find that the majority of recipes in this chapter are from the sweeter side of the spectrum. If I'm not blending up a smoothie for breakfast on a weekday, chances are I'm enjoying some oatmeal, granola with almond milk, chia porridge, or a quick-to-throw-together fruit and yogurt parfait.

On the weekends, I like to get a little fancier and make more time-consuming brunch dishes. Raw crêpes and "flaxjacks" (raw pancakes) require you to prep the night before, but you'll be richly rewarded when you wake up to these fragrant delights just begging to be paired with fruit, drizzled with chocolate or strawberry sauce, or smothered in Miso-Maple Butter.

Don't think I ignore the savory side, though! If you like saltier stuff for breakfast, I've got you covered. My Morning Mushroom Scramble is a great quick-fix dish for a weekday morning, while Biscuits and Sausage Gravy makes for a hearty weekend treat.

Le Matin Parfait (page 49), with Coconut Yogurt (page 50), Date-Nut Crumble (page 52); Apple Pie Oatmeal (page 56)

Breakfast Banana Split

YIELD: 2 SERVINGS

It may not be very traditional, but this variation on a banana split is like having dessert for breakfast! Treat yourself.

2 tablespoons Almond Butter (page 92)

2 teaspoons agave nectar

Pinch of sea salt

2 ripe bananas, peeled and halved lengthwise

1/2 cup Coconut Yogurt (page 50)

2 tablespoons Strawberry Coulis (page 94)

2 tablespoons Chocolate Silk Ganache (page 93)

1/4 cup chopped Continental Crunch Granola (page 51) (optional)

In a small bowl, stir together the almond butter, agave, and salt until smooth, adding a teaspoon of water if needed to blend. Set aside.

Place the halved bananas in two small serving dishes (two halves per dish). Spoon half the yogurt in the center of each dish. Drizzle half the almond butter-agave mixture on top of each, followed by the Strawberry Coulis and Chocolate Silk Ganache. Sprinkle the top of each with 2 tablespoons Continental Crunch Granola, if desired. Serve immediately.

Per serving: 449 calories, 23.5g sat (11g sat), 63.1g carbs, 9g fiber, 6g protein

SUBSTITUTIONS

- Almond Butter: cashew butter or peanut butter
- Agave nectar: coconut nectar, any other liquid sweetener, or 1 teaspoon filtered water plus stevia to taste
- Coconut Yogurt: store-bought nondairy yogurt
- Strawberry Coulis: Raspberry Jam (page 95)
- Continental Crunch Granola: Date-Nut Crumble (page 52) or any store-bought vegan granola

Le Matin Parfait

YIELD: 2 SERVINGS

Besides being a chef, I'm also a linguist, so sometimes I can't resist indulging in a little word-play. Americans know a parfait to be a cold dish or dessert made of alternating layers of fruit and cream. "Le matin" (roughly pronounced "luh mah-TAHN") is French for "morning," so in other words, this is a breakfast parfait. However, translated literally, the full phrase "le matin parfait" means "the perfect morning," which is what you'll have when you start your day with this parfait! I know, I'm a dork. (See photo, page 46.)

3/4 cup Coconut Yogurt (page 50)
1/2 cup Date-Nut Crumble (page 52)
3/4 cup fresh raspberries
3/4 cup fresh blackberries

Spoon about 2 tablespoons Coconut Yogurt into each of two parfait, wine, or highball glasses. Add 1 heaping tablespoon Date-Nut Crumble to each glass, then 2 tablespoons raspberries and 2 tablespoons blackberries. Repeat layers until all ingredients are used up. Serve immediately.

Per serving: 357 calories, 23.6g fat (10g sat), 38.7g carbs, 12g fiber, 4.7g protein

SUBSTITUTIONS

- Coconut Yogurt: store-bought nondairy yogurt
- Date-Nut Crumble: Continental Crunch Granola (page 51) or any store-bought vegan granola
- Berries: strawberries, blueberries, or chopped fresh fruit of any kind

GOT A CROWD?

To serve a crowd, simply quadruple this recipe and layer the elements in a glass trifle bowl for an elegant presentation.

Coconut Yogurt

YIELD: 4 SERVINGS (ABOUT 2 CUPS)

I never got into soy yogurt (something about it always tasted "off" to me), but from the first time I tried coconut yogurt, I was in love. This homemade version is even better than the ones at the store (and has far less sugar). (See photo, page 46.)

2 cups chopped young coconut meat

1 teaspoon probiotic powder (see page 17)

1 to 4 tablespoons coconut water

1 tablespoon agave nectar

1/2 teaspoon lemon juice

Pinch of sea salt

ADVANCE PREP

You will need to open and scrape the meat from 3 to 4 young Thai coconuts for this recipe. Reserve the extra coconut water for smoothies or other uses. (See page 31.)

Blend the coconut meat and probiotic powder in a high-speed blender, adding only as much of the coconut water as is needed to make the mixture very smooth (you may not need any at all). Transfer the mixture to a small bowl and cover it with plastic wrap. Place the bowl in a warm dehydrator or in the oven (making sure it is off) with the light turned on. Let sit for 6 to 8 hours or overnight to allow the yogurt to culture.

When the yogurt has finished culturing, transfer it back to the blender. Add the agave, lemon juice, and salt and blend briefly to combine. Transfer the yogurt back to a bowl and chill for at least 30 more minutes before serving.

Per 1/2 cup serving: 158 calories, 13.4g fat (12g sat), 10.4g carbs, 4g fiber, 1.4g protein

SUBSTITUTIONS

- Coconut water: filtered water
- Agave nectar: coconut nectar, any other liquid sweetener, or stevia to taste

VARIATIONS

Leave out the probiotic powder and skip the culturing step for a quick and easy non-fermented yogurt.

If you don't have access to fresh coconuts, make Cashew Yogurt instead by replacing the coconut meat with 1 1/3 cups cashews, soaked and drained, plus 2 tablespoons Coconut Butter (page 92) plus as much coconut water as is needed to blend (will make for a much richer yogurt).

Continental Crunch Granola

YIELD: 12 SERVINGS (ABOUT 6 CUPS)　CO

This is a great basic granola recipe that not only makes an awesome cereal (especially when topped with almond or hempseed milk), but can be jazzed up any way you like. Try adding 1/3 cup raw cacao powder to make chocolate granola, or a tablespoon or two of maca or mesquite powder to add superfood power.

1 1/2 cups raw rolled oat flakes or old-fashioned rolled oats

1 cup almonds, soaked for 8 to 12 hours and drained, roughly chopped

3/4 cup pecans, soaked for 4 to 6 hours and drained, roughly chopped

1/2 cup unsweetened flaked coconut

3/4 cup pitted dates, soaked for 15 to 30 minutes and drained

1/2 cup maple syrup

1 tablespoon lemon juice

2 teaspoons vanilla extract

1 teaspoon ground cinnamon

1/4 teaspoon sea salt

1/2 cup raisins

In a large bowl, mix together the oats, almonds, pecans, and coconut. Set aside.

In a food processor or high-speed blender, combine the dates, maple syrup, lemon juice, vanilla, cinnamon, and salt. Process until smooth, adding a splash of water if necessary to blend. Add the date mixture to the oat-nut mixture and stir thoroughly with a wooden spoon or spatula to combine.

Make It Raw: Spread the granola evenly across a mesh-lined dehydrator tray. Dehydrate for 20 to 24 hours, until completely dry. Once dried, mix in the raisins and store in the refrigerator.

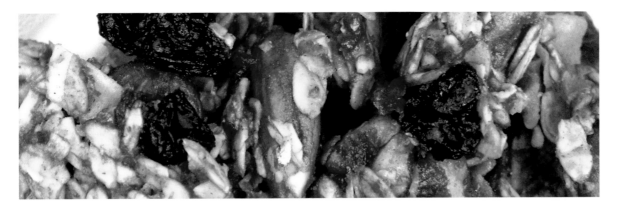

Make It Baked: Preheat the oven to 325°F and grease a baking sheet with coconut oil. Spread the granola evenly across the pan and bake for 25 to 30 minutes, stirring every 10 to 15 minutes, until crisp and lightly browned. Remove from the oven and let cool completely. Once cooled, mix in the raisins and store in an airtight container.

Per 1/2 cup serving: 227 calories, 10.8g fat (1.5g sat), 31.9g carbs, 4g fiber, 4.3g protein

SUBSTITUTIONS

- Almonds: hazelnuts
- Pecans: walnuts
- Raisins: dried cranberries, blueberries, or mulberries

Date-Nut Crumble

YIELD: 6 SERVINGS (ABOUT 1 1/2 CUPS)

This chewy-nutty-crumbly sweet topping is a cinch to put together and is amazing on top of just about anything—fruit, yogurt, oatmeal, you name it! It's hard for me not to just eat it with a spoon. (See photo, page 46.)

1/2 cup dry walnuts
1/2 cup dry pecans
Big pinch of sea salt
3/4 cup pitted dates

In a food processor, combine the walnuts, pecans, and salt and pulse until coarsely ground. Add the dates, a few at a time, pulsing several times between each addition, until fully incorporated. Store in the refrigerator.

Per 1/4 cup serving: 188 calories, 13.1g fat (1g sat), 18.6g carbs, 3g fiber, 3g protein

SUBSTITUTIONS

- Walnuts: almonds or additional pecans
- Pecans: almonds or additional walnuts
- Dates: raisins

Morning Mushroom Scramble

YIELD: 4 SIDE-DISH SERVINGS

As much as I like my sweet breakfasts, I sometimes crave a salty complement. This easy "scramble" can serve as a savory accompaniment to any other breakfast dish or can be enjoyed on its own. (Photo on page 63.)

1 cup dry almonds

1 teaspoon lemon juice

1/4 teaspoon garlic powder

1/4 teaspoon turmeric

1/4 teaspoon sea salt

1/4 cup filtered water

1/2 cup packed fresh spinach

1/2 batch Simple Seasoned Mushrooms (page 174)

Combine the almonds, lemon juice, garlic powder, turmeric, and salt in a food processor and pulse until the almonds are finely ground. Add the water and process until smooth. Add the spinach and pulse until well-incorporated. Add the Simple Seasoned Mushrooms and pulse until roughly chopped and just incorporated. Serve immediately.

Per serving: 148 calories, 12.9g fat (1g sat), 5.3g carbs, 3g fiber, 5.5g protein

SUBSTITUTIONS

- Almonds: sunflower seeds
- Simple Seasoned Mushrooms: 1 cup chopped crimini or button mushrooms plus 1 tablespoon tamari

VARIATION

Pulse in 2 to 4 tablespoons of nutritional yeast to make Cheesy Mushroom Scramble

INSTEAD OF MUSHROOMS

If you are not a fan of mushrooms, substitute diced bell pepper, grated carrot, or chopped cauliflower.

Chia Porridge with Blueberries

YIELD: 1 LARGE OR 2 SMALL SERVINGS

Chia seeds are one of nature's perfect foods, packed with protein, fiber, omega-3 essential fatty acids, protective antioxidants, and phytonutrients. Prepare this recipe the night before, storing the nuts and berries in a small baggie and the porridge in a container, then snatch it out of the fridge the next day on your way to work. This porridge has a loose consistency, but add more chia seeds if you prefer it thicker (see Variations, next page).

1 1/4 cups Almond Milk (page 30)
2 tablespoons chia seeds
4 pitted dates
1/4 teaspoon ground cinnamon
Pinch of sea salt
2 tablespoons dry pecans, chopped
1/2 cup fresh blueberries

The night before you plan to serve the porridge, combine the almond milk, chia seeds, dates, cinnamon, and salt in a high-speed blender and blend until smooth. Transfer the mixture to a container, cover, and refrigerate overnight to thicken.

The next morning, stir the nuts and blueberries into the porridge and serve chilled.

Per serving (if 2): 195 calories, 8.6g fat (1g sat), 28.9g carbs, 4g fiber, 3.8g protein

- Almond Milk: Coconut Milk (page 31) or any other nondairy milk
- Dates: 2 tablespoons raisins; 1 tablespoon maple syrup, agave nectar, coconut nectar, or any other liquid sweetener; or stevia to taste
- Pecans: walnuts or almonds
- Blueberries: any other berry or diced fruit

VARIATIONS

- Make "Power Porridge" by adding 2 tablespoons sprouted brown rice protein powder.
- Blend in 1/4 cup soaked and drained cashews for a richer porridge.
- Reduce the almond milk by 1/4 cup and blend in 1 extra tablespoon of chia seeds to create a thicker, more pudding-like consistency.
- Stir (don't blend) 1 extra tablespoon of chia seeds into the porridge just before refrigerating to add another dimension of texture.

Cold-Pressed Café au Lait

YIELD: 4 CUPS

A lot of raw foodists eschew coffee, but not I! If you enjoy a morning cup of joe, try cold-brewing it for a change using this method.

3 tablespoons ground coffee beans

3 cups cold filtered water

1 cup Almond Milk (page 30)

4 teaspoons agave nectar

Place the ground coffee in a 3-cup French press, add the cold water, and rest the lid on top. Let sit for 8 hours or overnight, then press the filter through the coffee.

In each of 4 cups or mugs, add 1/4 cup almond milk and 1 teaspoon agave. Top with the brewed coffee. Chill, if desired, and drink cold, or warm in the dehydrator for 1 hour or in a saucepan on the stove over low heat.

Per cup: 39 calories, .7g fat (trace sat), 7.8g carbs, 1g fiber, .7g protein

SUBSTITUTIONS

- Almond Milk: any other nondairy milk
- Agave nectar: coconut nectar, any other liquid sweetener, or stevia to taste

Apple Pie Oatmeal

YIELD: 2 SERVINGS   LF   CO   ‹30

This apple-pie-in-a-bowl oatmeal really hits the spot on a chilly morning. Oats contain beta-glucan, a soluble fiber that has been shown to reduce blood cholesterol levels by up to 10 percent—score! You get "extraw" credit if you make this with fresh-pressed apple juice and soaked, blended oat groats in place of the rolled oats (see the Variation below).

> 1 medium apple, peeled, cored, and chopped
> 1/2 cup Almond Milk (page 30)
> 1/2 cup apple juice
> 1 tablespoon maple syrup
> 3/4 teaspoon ground cinnamon
> 1/2 teaspoon vanilla extract
> Big pinch of sea salt
> 1 cup raw rolled oat flakes or old-fashioned rolled oats
> Additional almond milk, for serving (optional)

Combine all ingredients, except the oats and the optional additional almond milk, in a medium bowl. Add the oats and stir thoroughly to combine. Let sit for at least 10 minutes to allow the oats to soak up the liquid.

Serve cold, or warm in a dehydrator for 30 minutes or in a small saucepan on the stove over very low heat. Top with a splash of additional almond milk before serving, if desired.

Per serving: 270 calories, 3.9g fat (trace sat), 55.4g carbs, 6g fiber, 6.3g protein

SUBSTITUTIONS

- Almond Milk: any other nondairy milk
- Apple juice: filtered water plus 1 teaspoon agave nectar or stevia to taste
- Maple syrup: agave nectar, coconut nectar, any other liquid sweetener, or 1 tablespoon filtered water plus stevia to taste

VARIATION

To make "Groatmeal," soak 1 cup raw oat groats in filtered water for 12 to 24 hours. Rinse and drain the groats and transfer them to a food processor. Add all ingredients (omitting the oat flakes) except the apple, and process until smooth. Add the apple and pulse 2 to 3 times to incorporate. Serve cold, or warm in a dehydrator for 30 minutes or in a small saucepan on the stove over very low heat.

GLUTEN-FREE AND SOY-FREE DIETS

All of the recipes in this book are gluten-free and soy-free, as long as you take care in selecting the following ingredients:

Oats. Some of my recipes contain oats or oat flour, and although oats are gluten-free, they're often processed on gluten-contaminated equipment. If you have celiac disease or a sensitivity to traces of gluten on oats, be sure to purchase certified gluten-free oats and oat flour.

Tamari/soy sauce. Seek out a wheat-free brand of tamari, like Eden Foods or San-J.

Miso. If you avoid soy products, opt for chickpea or barley miso instead of soy-based varieties.

Flaxjacks with Miso-Maple Butter

YIELD: 4 SERVINGS (2 PANCAKES PER SERVING)

Oh. My. Goodness. You've never tasted raw pancakes until you've had these babies. They're not much like cooked pancakes, but instead have a delightfully chewy texture all their own. These "flaxjacks" are lightly sweetened and banana-bread-scented, and the Miso-Maple Butter I top them with may just be the most melt-in-your-mouth, I-want-to-eat-a-whole-jar-of-this spread you've ever tasted. You've been warned.

For the pancakes:

1 large, very ripe banana, peeled
1 large ripe pear, peeled, cored, and chopped
1/2 cup cashews, soaked for 2 to 4 hours and drained
2 tablespoons maple syrup
1 tablespoon melted coconut oil
1/2 teaspoon lemon juice
Pinch of sea salt
1/4 cup ground flaxseed

ADVANCE PREP

The pancakes need to be prepared the night before you plan to serve them.

For the Miso-Maple Butter:

1/4 cup Coconut Butter (page 92)
2 tablespoons maple syrup
1/2 teaspoon white miso

To serve:

Additional maple syrup, nut butter of choice, and/or Raspberry Jam (page 95) (optional)

For the pancakes: Combine all ingredients except the flaxseed in a high-speed blender or food processor. Blend until completely smooth. Add the flax and blend again briefly, until just incorporated.

Spoon the pancake batter, a scant 1/4 cup at a time, onto a Teflex-lined dehydrator tray. Spread gently with the back of the spoon to create a circular shape, about 1/3 inch thick. Repeat with all remaining batter (you should end up with about 8 pancakes). Dehydrate for 8 hours or overnight, until dry on top but still tender. Peel the pancakes from the Teflex sheet, turn them over, and dehydrate for about 1 more hour.

For the Miso-Maple Butter: Whisk together the coconut butter, maple syrup, and miso in a small bowl. Mixture will be thick.

Serve the pancakes warm with the Miso-Maple Butter and additional syrup, nut butter, or jam, if desired.

Per serving: 343 calories, 23.4g fat (13g sat), 32.6g carbs, 6g fiber, 5.8g protein

SUBSTITUTIONS

- Pear: apple
- Flax: finely ground chia seeds
- Maple syrup: agave nectar, coconut nectar, any other liquid sweetener, or 1 tablespoon filtered water plus stevia to taste
- Miso: big pinch of sea salt

COOKED VARIATION

This mixture does not cook or bake well, so instead, whip up a batch of your favorite cooked pancakes and top those with the divine Miso-Maple Butter.

Parisian Street Crêpes

YIELD: 6 SERVINGS (2 CRÊPES PER SERVING)   `LF`

I'll never forget the crêpe I ate in Paris when I spent five weeks in Europe in 2009...in other words, crêpes are memorable! Anyone you serve these to is sure to ooh and ahh over them. You'll need to remember to prep the crêpes the night before, but they're so very worth the extra planning. You can fill them with just about anything you please, too—try nut butters, or different fruits, or any of the other sweet sauces in the Cheeses, Spreads, & Sauces *chapter.*

For the crêpes:

1 medium zucchini, peeled and chopped (1 1/2 to 2 cups)

1 large ripe mango, peeled, seeded, and chopped

1 tablespoon agave nectar

1 teaspoon lemon juice

1/4 teaspoon vanilla extract

Pinch of sea salt

1/4 cup ground flaxseed

ADVANCE PREP
The crepes need to be prepared the night before you plan to serve them.

To serve:

1 1/2 cups strawberries, hulled and chopped

1/4 cup Chocolate Silk Ganache (page 93)

1/4 cup Strawberry Coulis (page 94)

For the crêpes: Combine all ingredients except the flaxseed in a high-speed blender or food processor. Blend until completely smooth. Add the flax and blend again briefly, until just incorporated.

Spoon the batter, a scant 1/4 cup at a time, onto a Teflex-lined dehydrator tray. Spread gently with the back of the spoon to create a very thin circle, about 1/8 to 1/4 inch thick. Repeat with all remaining batter (you should end up with about 12 crêpes). Dehydrate for 8 hours or overnight, until dry but still pliable. (If the crêpes overdried a little, that's ok—just spray or brush them with some water to get them pliable again.)

To serve: Roll 2 tablespoons chopped strawberries into each crêpe wrapper. Drizzle Chocolate Silk Ganache and Strawberry Coulis on top of the rolled crêpes.

Per serving: 131 calories, 4.9g fat (2g sat), 22.9g carbs, 5g fiber, 2.1g protein

- Agave nectar: coconut nectar, any other liquid sweetener, or stevia to taste
- Flax: finely ground chia seeds
- Strawberries: sliced bananas

COOKED VARIATION

This mixture does not cook or bake well, so instead, whip up a batch of your favorite cooked crêpes and top those with the strawberries, Chocolate Silk Ganache, and Strawberry Coulis.

Biscuits and Sausage Gravy

YIELD: 4 SERVINGS `CO`

I've long been a fan of baked vegan biscuits and white bean-based gravy, but a raw version was new territory for me. Luckily, the mild Buckwheat-Oat Biscuits (page 74) are excellent when split and topped with this cheesy cashew-based gravy dotted with nutmeat "sausage."

For the "sausage":
1/2 cup dry walnuts
1 teaspoon tamari
1/2 teaspoon fennel seeds
1/2 teaspoon dried sage
1/4 teaspoon garlic powder
For the gravy:
1/2 cup cashews, soaked for 2 to 4 hours and drained
1/3 cup filtered water
1/4 cup nutritional yeast
2 teaspoons lemon juice
1/4 teaspoon sea salt
To serve:
1/2 batch Buckwheat-Oat Biscuits (4 biscuits, or 8 biscuit halves) (page 74)
Freshly cracked black pepper (optional)

For the "sausage" crumbles: Combine the walnuts, tamari, fennel seeds, sage, and garlic powder in a food processor and pulse until coarsely ground. Set aside.

For the gravy: Combine the cashews, water, nutritional yeast, lemon juice, and salt in a high-speed blender and blend until very smooth. Transfer the gravy to a medium bowl and gently fold in the "sausage" crumbles (don't overmix).

To serve: Use a sharp knife to cut the biscuits in half lengthwise (like a bagel) if they are not already halved. Divide the biscuit halves, cut-side up, among 4 plates and top generously with the sausage gravy. Sprinkle with black pepper before serving, if desired.

Per serving: 322 calories, 20.3g fat (2g sat), 28.5g carbs, 7g fiber, 11.5g protein

SUBSTITUTIONS

- Tamari: soy sauce, nama shoyu, or liquid aminos
- Buckwheat-Oat Biscuits: your favorite homemade or store-bought baked biscuits

Breads & Crackers

Let's talk about bread. I've always been a carboholic; more specifically, a fiend for bread. My appetite for it is endless—if there is any bread in front of me, I will eat it. As such, I pretty much never buy it. Let's face it: overdosing on grain, gluten, and sodium is pretty darn tasty. Unfortunately, our bodies just don't love it as much as our taste buds do.

Enter: raw breads. Free of refined flours, wheat, and gluten—and filled with plant protein, fiber, and healthy fats—raw breads are a boon to anyone struggling with carbophilia. That said, I'll tell you up front: raw breads have a taste and texture all their own. With no yeast or leavening agents, they're much denser than baked breads. If you have access to Irish moss gel (see page 23), include it in your breads whenever possible, as it'll lend an irresistible fluffiness you have to taste to believe.

Raw crackers are another wonderful snack to have on hand. Use them to scoop up dips and cheeses or simply to munch on plain. Store all breads and crackers in airtight containers in the refrigerator.

Zesty Corn Tortilla Chips (page 78), Garden Fresh Salsa (page 89)

Rosemary-Garlic Bread

YIELD: 8 PIECES   `CO`

The heavenly aroma of this bread will fill your kitchen as it dehydrates. I love to serve it along-side Spaghetti alla Marinara (page 136), Spinach-Walnut Pesto Pasta (page 138), or Vermicelli with Pecan Cream Sauce (page 142).

1 medium zucchini, peeled and chopped (1 1/2 to 2 cups)
1 tablespoon lemon juice
2 pitted dates, minced
1 clove garlic, peeled
1 teaspoon dried rosemary
1 teaspoon sea salt
1 1/2 cups almond flour
1/2 cup oat flour
1/4 cup ground flaxseed
1/4 cup filtered water

Combine the zucchini, lemon juice, dates, garlic, rosemary, and salt in a food processor and blend until smooth. Add the flours, flax, and water and pulse until a sticky dough forms.

Make It Raw: Spoon the dough in 8 portions onto a Teflex-lined dehydrator tray. Using a spoon or your hands (moistened with water), shape the mixture into 8 small loaves or ovals about 3/4 inch thick. Dehydrate for about 2 hours, until dry on top, then flip over onto a mesh-lined tray and peel off the Teflex sheet. Dehydrate for 6 to 8 more hours, until dry and firm.

Make It Baked: Preheat the oven to 350°F and grease a baking sheet with coconut oil. Spoon the dough in 8 portions onto the baking sheet. Using a spoon or your hands (moistened with water), shape the mixture into 8 small loaves or ovals about 3/4 inch thick. Bake for about 15 minutes, until dry on top. Remove from the oven and carefully flip over with a spatula. Bake for about 15 more minutes, until dry and lightly browned. (The interior of this bread will remain very moist.) Remove from the oven and let cool completely before serving.

Per piece: 172 calories, 12.4g fat (1g sat), 11.9g carbs, 4g fiber, 6.4g protein

SUBSTITUTIONS

- Zucchini: yellow squash
- Dates: 2 tablespoons raisins or golden raisins

- Almond flour: any other nut flour
- Oat flour: buckwheat flour
- Flax: finely ground chia seeds

VARIATION

Blend 1/4 to 1/2 cup Irish moss gel (see page 23) into the zucchini mixture to create a beautifully fluffy bread.

Naansense Bread

YIELD: 8 PIECES

A single large Brazil nut contains over 100 percent of the daily dietary requirement of selenium, an essential trace mineral with cancer-fighting qualities. This Indian-inspired flatbread is so good, you'll want to snack on it naanstop. Top it with Mango Chutney (page 90) for a sweet 'n salty treat. (See photo, page 159.)

1 cup dry Brazil nuts
1 small clove garlic, peeled
1 small zucchini, peeled and chopped (about 1 cup)
1/2 cup chopped young coconut meat
1/2 cup almond flour
1 tablespoon lemon juice
2 pitted dates, minced
1 1/2 teaspoons salt
1/2 cup ground flaxseed

Place the Brazil nuts and garlic in a food processor and pulse until finely ground. Add the zucchini, coconut meat, almond flour, lemon juice, dates, and salt, and process until all ingredients are combined and fairly smooth. Add the flax and pulse until incorporated.

Make It Raw: Using a spoon or small offset spatula, spread the mixture into 8 small ovals (about 1/4 to 1/3 inch thick) on a Teflex-lined dehydrator tray. Dehydrate for 1 to 2 hours, until dry on top, then flip over onto a mesh-lined tray and peel off the Teflex sheet. Dehydrate for 4 to 6 more hours, until dry and firm.

Make It Baked: Preheat the oven to 300°F and grease a baking sheet with coconut oil. Using a spoon or small offset spatula, spread the mixture into 8 small ovals (about 1/4 to 1/3 inch thick) on the baking sheet. Bake for about 10 to 12 minutes, until dry on top. Remove from the oven and carefully flip over with a spatula. Bake for about 8 to 10 more minutes, until dry and lightly browned. Remove from the oven and let cool before serving.

Per piece: 219 calories, 19.8g fat (5g sat), 8.9g carbs, 4g fiber, 5.7g protein

SUBSTITUTIONS

- Brazil nuts: almonds or hazelnuts
- Coconut meat: 1/4 cup Coconut Butter (page 92) plus 1/4 cup filtered water
- Almond flour: any other nut flour or buckwheat flour
- Flax: finely ground chia seeds

VARIATION

Blend 1/4 cup Irish moss gel (see page 23) into the batter to create a more airy texture.

Banana Bread Squares

YIELD: 6 SLICES

These thin, chewy, no-sugar-added slices of banana bread make a perfect snack, especially when topped with almond or coconut butter. Try them also in the Open-Faced Nutty Butter Sandwiches on page 149.

3 large (or 4 small) very ripe bananas, peeled
2 teaspoons lemon juice
1/2 teaspoon vanilla extract
Pinch of sea salt
3/4 cup almond flour
2 tablespoons ground flaxseed
1 tablespoon melted coconut oil

Combine the bananas, lemon juice, vanilla, and salt in a high-speed blender or food processor and blend until smooth. Add the almond flour and flax and blend to combine. With the machine running, pour in the coconut oil in a thin stream and blend until incorporated. (The batter will be very thin.)

Make It Raw: Pour the mixture onto a Teflex-lined dehydrator tray. With an offset spatula, smooth the batter evenly into a square or rectangle at least 1/3 inch thick. Dehydrate for 4 to 6 hours, until the top looks dry, then carefully flip over onto a mesh-lined tray and peel off the Teflex sheet. Dehydrate an additional 2 to 4 hours, until dry to the touch. Slide the bread onto a work surface and cut it into 6 squares, placing them back on the mesh tray. Dehydrate for 8 more hours or overnight.

Make It Baked: Preheat the oven to 325°F and grease a baking sheet with coconut oil. Spoon the batter onto the baking sheet in 6 portions, then spread each into a circle or square shape at least 1/3 inch thick with an offset spatula. Bake for 10 minutes, remove from the oven, and carefully flip each piece over with a spatula. Bake for about 8 more minutes, then transfer the bread to a wire rack to cool.

Per slice: 167 calories, 10.5g fat (3g sat), 17.6g carbs, 4g fiber, 4g protein

SUBSTITUTIONS

- Almond flour: any other nut flour
- Flax: finely ground chia seeds

VARIATION

Stir 1/4 cup finely chopped walnuts into the batter before spreading onto the tray or baking sheet.

Apple-Cinnamon Raisin Bread

YIELD: 8 SLICES

This super-moist bread makes a great snack or breakfast, especially when spread with your favorite nut butter!

2 large apples, peeled, cored, and chopped
1/4 cup agave nectar
2 tablespoons melted coconut oil
1 tablespoon lemon juice
2 teaspoons ground cinnamon
1/4 teaspoon sea salt
1 cup almond flour
1/2 cup ground flaxseed
1/2 cup raisins

Combine the apples, agave, coconut oil, lemon juice, cinnamon, and salt in a food processor and blend until smooth. Add the flour and flax and pulse until a sticky dough forms. Stir (or briefly pulse) in the raisins.

Make It Raw: Pour the mixture onto a Teflex-lined dehydrator tray. With an offset spatula, smooth the batter evenly into a square or rectangle about 3/4 inch thick. Dehydrate for 4 hours, then flip over onto a mesh-lined tray and peel off the Teflex sheet. Dehydrate for about 8 to 10 more hours or overnight, until dry on the surface but still tender to the touch.

Make It Baked: Preheat the oven to 350°F and grease a baking sheet with coconut oil. Spoon the batter onto the baking sheet in 4 portions, then use a spoon or offset spatula to spread each portion into a rectangle about 3/4-inch thick. Bake for about 15 minutes, until dry on top, then remove from the oven and carefully flip each piece over with a spatula. Bake for 5 to 10 more minutes, then transfer the bread to a wire rack to cool before cutting each rectangle into two slices.

Per slice: 226 calories, 13.5g fat (4g sat), 26.1g carbs, 6g fiber, 4.7g protein

SUBSTITUTIONS

- Agave nectar: coconut nectar or any other liquid sweetener
- Almond flour: any other nut flour
- Flax: finely ground chia seeds

VARIATIONS

- Blend 1/4 cup Irish moss gel (see page 23) into the apple mixture to make a lighter, fluffier bread.
- Add 1/4 cup finely chopped walnuts to the batter along with the raisins.

Nut and Seed Flatbread

YIELD: 12 SLICES   `CO`

This satisfying bread is low in carbohydrates and high in protein, fiber, essential minerals, and healthy fats. Its mild flavor allows it to be topped with anything you please, from nut cheese to nut butter.

> 1 cup ground flaxseed
> 1/3 cup whole flaxseeds
> 1/3 cup sunflower seeds, dry or soaked and drained
> 1/3 cup almond flour
> 2 tablespoons sesame seeds
> 2 tablespoons hempseeds
> 3/4 teaspoon sea salt
> 1 cup filtered water

In a medium bowl, mix all ingredients except water. Add the water and mix with a wooden spoon until combined. Let the batter sit for 3 to 5 minutes to allow the flaxseeds to gel.

Make It Raw: Using a spoon or offset spatula, spread the mixture evenly in a large square or rectangle about 1/2-inch thick on a Teflex-lined dehydrator tray. Dehydrate for about 2 hours, until dry on top, then flip over onto a mesh-lined tray and peel off the Teflex sheet. Using a sharp knife, score it into 12 pieces. Dehydrate for about 2 to 4 more hours, until dry but still slightly pliable, and then break into individual slices.

Make It Baked: Preheat the oven to 325°F and grease a baking sheet with coconut oil. Using a spoon or small offset spatula, spread the mixture evenly in a large square or rectangle about 1/3 to 1/2 inch thick on the baking sheet. Bake for about 15 minutes, until dry on top, then remove from the oven and carefully flip over with a spatula. With a sharp knife, score the bread into 12 slices and return the pan to the oven. Bake for about 10 more minutes, until dry and lightly browned. Remove from the oven and let cool completely before breaking into individual slices.

Per slice: 132 calories, 10.6g fat (1g sat), 6.2g carbs, 5g fiber, 5g protein

SUBSTITUTIONS

- Sunflower seeds: chopped pumpkin seeds or almonds
- Almond flour: any other nut flour, buckwheat flour, or oat flour
- Hempseeds: additional sesame seeds

For Cheesy-Garlic Flatbread, add 1/4 cup nutritional yeast, 1/2 teaspoon garlic powder, and 1 extra tablespoon of filtered water to the batter.

Nut and Seed Flatbread (opposite) alternating with Rosemary-Garlic Bread slices (page 66)

Buckwheat-Oat Biscuits

YIELD: 8 BISCUITS   `LF` `CO`

Buckwheat is a gluten-free "pseudograin" high in complete protein, iron, and zinc. I combine buckwheat flour with nutritious oat flour (see pages 21-22 for how to make your own flours) to create these basic biscuits. They're intentionally bland to allow them to be a canvas for a variety of appetizing toppings. Smother them with "sausage" gravy (page 62), or try one with Coconut Butter (page 92) and Raspberry Jam (page 95)—yum!

1 cup buckwheat flour

3/4 cup oat flour

1/4 cup ground flaxseed

1/2 teaspoon sea salt

1 tablespoon agave nectar

1 cup filtered water

In a food processor, combine the flours, flax, and salt, and pulse to combine. Add the agave and water and blend until a sticky dough forms.

Make It Raw: Spoon the dough in 8 portions onto a Teflex-lined dehydrator tray. Using a spoon or your hands (moistened with water), shape the mixture into 8 biscuits and press down lightly on each one to flatten it. Dehydrate for 2 to 4 hours, until dry on top, then flip over onto a mesh-lined tray and peel off the Teflex sheet. Dehydrate for about 6 more hours, until dry and firm. Use a sharp knife to cut the biscuits in half lengthwise (like you would cut a bagel)—they should be tender inside, but not wet. If the inside is still wet, return the biscuit halves to the dehydrator, cut side up, and dehydrate for an additional 2 to 4 hours, until the centers feel dry.

Make It Baked: Preheat the oven to 350°F and grease a baking sheet with coconut oil. Spoon the dough in 8 portions onto the baking sheet. Using a spoon or your hands (moistened with water), shape the mixture into 8 biscuits and press down slightly on each one to flatten it. Bake for 5 to 7 minutes, until dry on top, then remove from the oven and let cool slightly (do not turn off the oven). When cool enough to handle, use a sharp knife to cut the biscuits in half lengthwise (like you would cut a bagel). Return to the oven and bake for about 3 more minutes, until dry and lightly browned. Remove from the oven and let cool completely.

Per biscuit: 110 calories, 2.5g fat (trace sat), 19.2g carbs, 4g fiber, 4.1g protein

- Flax: finely ground chia seeds
- Agave nectar: coconut nectar or any other liquid sweetener

VARIATION

Blend 1/4 to 1/2 cup Irish moss gel (see page 23) into the dough to create light, fluffy biscuits.

Basic Flax Crackers

YIELD: 6 SERVINGS

Flaxseed's high content of omega-3 fats, fiber, and plant lignans make it an all-around cancer-fighter. These simple, bare crackers are the perfect vehicle for rich raw cheeses or other dips and spreads beginning on page 81.

1 cup ground flaxseed
1/4 cup whole flaxseeds
1 tablespoon tamari
1 teaspoon lemon juice
2/3 cup filtered water
1/2 teaspoon sea salt, for sprinkling

In a medium bowl, mix all ingredients except water and sea salt. Add the water and mix with a wooden spoon until combined. Let the batter sit for 3 to 5 minutes to allow the flaxseeds to gel. (Stir in 1 to 2 tablespoons more water if the batter looks too thick to spread.)

Make It Raw: Using a spoon or offset spatula, spread the mixture evenly in a large square or rectangle about 1/8 to 1/4 inch thick on a Teflex-lined dehydrator tray. Sprinkle evenly with the salt. Dehydrate for about 2 hours, until dry on top, then flip over onto a mesh-lined tray and peel off the Teflex sheet. Using a sharp knife, score into small cracker-size squares. Dehydrate about 6 to 8 more hours or overnight, until dry on top, then break into individual crackers. Place the crackers back on the mesh-lined tray and dehydrate for 12 to 24 more hours, or until crisp.

Make It Baked: Preheat the oven to 325°F and grease a baking sheet with coconut oil. Using a spoon or small offset spatula, spread the mixture evenly in a large square or rectangle about 1/8 to 1/4 inch thick on the baking sheet. Sprinkle evenly with the salt. Bake for about 10 minutes, until dry on top. Remove from the oven and carefully flip over onto a work surface with a spatula. Let cool for 2 to 3 minutes, then trim edges (if desired) and slice into small cracker-size squares, returning them to the baking sheet. Reduce the heat to 300°F and bake for about 10 more minutes, until crisp. Remove from the oven and let cool completely.

Per serving: 141 calories, 10.6g fat (1g sat), 8.4g carbs, 7g fiber, 5.3g protein

SUBSTITUTIONS

- Tamari: soy sauce, nama shoyu, or liquid aminos

VARIATION

For Cheesy Flax Crackers, add 1/4 cup nutritional yeast and 2 extra tablespoons of filtered water to the batter.

Mediterranean Herbed Crackers

YIELD: 6 SERVINGS

You can flavor your flax crackers in just about any way, but I'm partial to this Italian-inspired variation. I like to spread them with dabs of Basil-Parsley Pesto (page 91) or Olive Tapenade-Stuffed Cheese (page 84) for a flavor-packed snack.

1 cup ground flaxseed
1/4 cup whole flaxseed
1 small clove garlic, peeled
1 teaspoon lemon juice
1 teaspoon balsamic vinegar
1 teaspoon dried basil
1 teaspoon dried oregano
1 teaspoon sea salt
3/4 cup filtered water

In a medium bowl, mix all ingredients except water. Add the water and mix with a wooden spoon until combined. Let the batter sit for 3 to 5 minutes to allow the flaxseeds to gel. (Stir in 1 to 2 tablespoons more water if the batter looks too thick to spread.)

Make It Raw: Using a spoon or offset spatula, spread the mixture evenly in a large square or rectangle about 1/8 to 1/4 inch thick on a Teflex-lined dehydrator tray. Dehydrate for about 2 hours, until dry on top, then flip over onto a mesh-lined tray and peel off the

Teflex sheet. Using a sharp knife, score into small cracker-size squares. Dehydrate 6 to 8 more hours or overnight, until dry on top, then break into individual crackers. Place the crackers back on the mesh-lined tray and dehydrate for 12 to 24 more hours, or until crisp.

Make It Baked: Preheat the oven to 325°F and grease a baking sheet with coconut oil. Using a spoon or small offset spatula, spread the mixture evenly in a large square or rectangle about 1/8 to 1/4 inch thick on the baking sheet. Bake for about 10 minutes, until dry on top. Remove from the oven and carefully flip over onto a work surface with a spatula. Let cool for 2 to 3 minutes, then trim edges (if desired) and slice into small cracker-size squares, returning them to the baking sheet. Reduce the heat to 300°F and bake for about 10 more minutes, until crisp. Remove from the oven and let cool completely.

Per serving: 141 calories, 10.6g fat (1g sat), 8.6g carbs, 7g fiber, 5g protein

SUBSTITUTIONS

- Balsamic vinegar: lemon juice
- Basil and oregano: 2 teaspoons Italian seasoning

Graham Crackers

YIELD: 6 SERVINGS

These lightly sweetened graham crackers are great to snack on plain, but try dipping them in Vanilla Bean Crème (page 93) or Chocolate Silk Ganache (page 93) for a real treat. The crackers are rather delicate, so if you end up with some crumbled ones, try using them like vanilla wafers in a pudding parfait, perhaps with Just-Like-Grandma's Banana Pudding (page 221) or Spiced Pumpkin Spooncream (page 222)!

1 cup almond flour

1/2 cup coconut flour

1/4 cup coconut palm sugar

2 tablespoons ground flaxseed

1 tablespoon agave nectar

1 teaspoon vanilla extract

1 teaspoon ground cinnamon

Pinch of sea salt

1 cup filtered water

In a food processor, combine all ingredients except water; process until combined. Add the water and pulse until the mixture is sticky and well-combined. Add additional water, a tablespoon at a time, if necessary to help the mixture blend.

Make It Raw: Using a spoon or your hands (moistened with water), spread the mixture evenly in a large square or rectangle about 1/8 to 1/4 inch thick on a Teflex-lined dehydrator tray. (Alternatively, place the dough between two Teflex sheets and use a rolling pin to flatten it.) Dehydrate for about 2 hours, until dry on top, then flip over onto a mesh-lined tray and peel off the Teflex sheet. Using a sharp knife, score into cracker-size squares. Dehydrate for 4 to 6 more hours or overnight, until dry, then break into individual crackers.

Make It Baked: Preheat the oven to 325°F and grease a baking sheet with coconut oil. Using a spoon or small offset spatula, spread the mixture evenly in a large square or rectangle about 1/8 to 1/4 inch thick on the baking sheet. Bake for 12 to 15 minutes, until dry on top. Remove from the oven and carefully flip over with a spatula (they may break; that's OK). With a sharp knife, score into cracker-size squares or rectangles. Reduce the heat to 300°F and bake for about 10 to 12 more minutes, until crisped and browned at the edges. Remove from the oven and let cool completely.

Per serving: 169 calories, 11.2g fat (1g sat), 15.7g carbs, 5g fiber, 5.1g protein

SUBSTITUTIONS

- Almond flour: oat flour, or buckwheat flour
- Coconut flour: additional almond flour (reducing the amount of water to 1/2 cup)
- Coconut palm sugar: brown sugar (not packed), Sucanat, date sugar, or maple sugar
- Flax: finely ground chia seeds
- Agave nectar: maple syrup, coconut nectar, or any other liquid sweetener

Zesty Corn Tortilla Chips

YIELD: 8 SERVINGS

These party-friendly corn chips are a great match for Garden Fresh Salsa (page 89) or Garlicky Guacamole (page 88). Save some to crumble on top of a Taco Salad Supreme (page 128), too! (See photo, page 64.)

4 cups frozen corn, thawed
1 medium yellow or red bell pepper, seeded and chopped

1 medium zucchini, peeled and chopped (1 1/2 to 2 cups)
1 tablespoon lime juice
2 teaspoons chili powder
1 teaspoon ground cumin
1 teaspoon ground coriander
1 teaspoon sea salt
1/4 teaspoon cayenne pepper (optional)
1 1/2 cups ground flaxseed

In a high-speed blender or food processor, combine all ingredients except flax and blend until smooth. Add the flax and blend briefly, until incorporated (add a splash of water if necessary).

With an offset spatula, spread the mixture thinly and evenly onto two Teflex-lined dehydrator trays. Dehydrate for about 2 hours, until dry on top, then flip each over onto a mesh-lined tray and dehydrate for 1 to 2 more hours. Slide each flat of chips onto a work surface and cut into triangles with a sharp knife. Transfer the cut chips back to the mesh-lined trays and dehydrate up to 24 to 48 hours, until dry and crisp.

Per serving: 195 calories, 9.7g fat (1g sat), 25.1g carbs, 8g fiber, 6.9g protein

SUBSTITUTIONS

- Zucchini: yellow squash
- Lime juice: lemon juice

VARIATION

Spread the mixture into 8 thin rounds on the two Teflex-lined dehydrator trays and halve all the dehydration times to create flexible corn tortillas.

COOKED VARIATION

This mixture does not bake well, so instead, grab a package of storebought corn tortillas and preheat the oven to 350°F. Grease a baking sheet with coconut oil and cut the tortillas into wedges or strips. In a large bowl, toss the tortilla pieces with the lime juice, chili powder, cumin, coriander, sea salt, and cayenne, if desired, in the amounts listed above. Spread the chips evenly on the baking sheet in a single layer and bake for 8 to 12 minutes (depending on the thickness of the tortillas), or until golden brown, watching them closely to make sure they don't burn.

⌒ Cheeses, Spreads, & Sauces

||||||||||||||||||||||||||||||||||||||||||||||||||||||||||||||||||||||||||||||||||||||||||||||||||||||

Cheese was never a food I enjoyed, even when I ate dairy products, so I had no problem banning it from my diet altogether. Truth be told, I'm not even much of a fan of store-bought vegan cheeses. But raw cheeses changed my views on cheese forever. If you, like most people I know, are prone to cheese cravings, look no further than these easy, delicious, nut-based recipes. You can even make them without probiotic powder, though including it will give you the most authentic, tangy, cultured flavor. If you like firmer cheeses, you can dehydrate the finished cheeses for several hours or overnight to create a rind on the edges. In an airtight container, raw cheeses can be stored in the fridge for up to a month, if not even longer.

The rest of this chapter is packed with all manner of spreads, sauces, dips, drizzles, relishes, and toppings, both savory and sweet. You'll find many of them called for in other recipes in this book, where they serve to enhance both the taste and presentation of anything they grace.

(from left) Balsamic-Fig Pistachio Cheese (page 85), Olive Tapenade-Stuffed Cheese (page 84), and Mexican Cheddar Cheese (page 83)

Basic Nut Cheese

YIELD: ABOUT 1 CUP

Probiotics are "friendly bacteria" that aid digestion, support the immune system, and help maintain a healthy balance of intestinal microflora. They're abundant in cultured and fermented foods such as yogurt, miso, kimchi, kefir, kombucha, and nut cheeses. That's right—raw nut cheeses such as the ones that follow are actually good for you!

1 cup macadamia nuts or cashews, soaked for 2 to 4 hours and drained
1/2 cup filtered water
1/2 teaspoon probiotic powder (see page 17)
1 teaspoon nutritional yeast
1/2 teaspoon lemon juice
1/2 teaspoon sea salt

Combine the nuts, water, and probiotic powder in a high-speed blender and blend until completely smooth. Line a strainer or colander with a double layer of cheesecloth, letting the excess cheesecloth hang over the sides. Place the strainer over a large bowl and pour the cheese mixture into the cheesecloth, then fold the excess over the cheese so it is covered. Place a weight on top that is heavy enough to gently compress the cheese without pushing it through the cheesecloth. Place the bowl with the strainer on the countertop for 24 hours to allow the cheese to culture at room temperature.

After at least 24 (and no more than 48) hours, take the cheese out of the strainer and unwrap it from the cheesecloth, placing it in a small bowl. Add the nutritional yeast, lemon juice, and salt and stir thoroughly with a wooden spoon to incorporate. Place in the refrigerator to chill for at least 8 hours or overnight before using.

Per 2 tablespoon serving: 110 calories, 10.2g fat (2g sat), 3.9g carbs, 1g fiber, 2.3g protein

SUBSTITUTIONS

- Macadamia nuts or cashews: Brazil nuts, almonds, hazelnuts, pistachios, or any other nut

VARIATION

Leave out the probiotic powder and skip the culturing step (letting the cheesecloth-wrapped cheese drain overnight in the refrigerator instead of on the countertop) to make non-fermented cheese.

Mexican Cheddar Cheese

YIELD: ABOUT 1 CUP

This might just be my favorite cheese of the bunch! With its winning blend of spices, it'll have you saying "¡Olé!" at first bite. It's a great addition to Fiesta Taco Roll-Ups (page 162), but it's also divine when spread on simple Basic Flax Crackers (page 75) and allowed to shine. (See photo, page 80.)

1 batch Basic Nut Cheese (page 82), made with macadamia nuts

1 1/2 teaspoons chili powder

1 teaspoon nutritional yeast

1 teaspoon ground cumin

1/2 teaspoon ground coriander

1/4 teaspoon onion powder

1/4 teaspoon garlic powder

1/8 teaspoon cayenne pepper (optional)

Combine all ingredients in a medium bowl and stir well to combine. (Alternatively, use a food processor to blend all the ingredients together.) Shape into a small round on a plate (using a ring mold, if desired) and refrigerate until firm.

Per 2 tablespoon serving: 114 calories, 10.4g fat (2g sat), 4.4g carbs, 1g fiber, 2.5g protein

SOAKING NUTS AND SEEDS

Soaking nuts and seeds is not an optional step in raw food recipes; it's a requirement! Nuts and seeds soften a great deal when soaked, resulting in a creamier texture and smoother mouth-feel when they're blended. Before making a recipe, be sure to scan the ingredient list in advance, taking note of any nuts or seeds that need to be soaked ahead of time. Consult the chart on page 21 for a complete list of soaking times and details on the proper soaking method.

If you're really short on time, here are a couple tricks for speeding up the soaking process:

- Soak the nuts or seeds in very warm (but not hot) water instead of cold.
- Place the bowl in the dehydrator to keep the water warm while soaking.
- In lieu of using a dehydrator, drain the nuts or seeds frequently (every 20 to 30 minutes) and replace the soak water with fresh warm water each time.

With a combination of those techniques, you can get away with soaking nuts and seeds in about half the recommended time.

Olive Tapenade-Stuffed Cheese

YIELD: ABOUT 1 1/4 CUPS

This layered cheese makes for an impressive party presentation. The salty, ultra-flavorful Kalamata olive tapenade is the perfect complement to mild macadamia cheese. (See photo, page 80.)

    1 tablespoon olive oil
    1 tablespoon lemon juice
    1/2 teaspoon miso paste
    1/2 cup pitted Kalamata olives
    1 tablespoon capers, rinsed (optional)
    1/2 small clove garlic, peeled
    1 batch Basic Nut Cheese (page 82), made with macadamia nuts

In a small bowl, whisk together the oil, lemon juice, and miso. In a small food processor (or by hand with a knife), pulse the olives, capers, and garlic until chunky. Add the olive mixture to the bowl with the oil mixture and stir to combine.

Spoon half the cheese onto a plate and spread into a small circle. (You can use a ring mold if you like.) Spoon 3/4 of the tapenade onto the cheese and press it down gently, then carefully top with the remaining half of the cheese. Top with the last 1/4 of the tapenade. Serve immediately or refrigerate until the cheese is firm.

Per 2 tablespoon serving: 114 calories, 10.6g fat (1g sat), 4.4g carbs, 1g fiber, 2g protein

SUBSTITUTIONS

- Miso: pinch of sea salt
- Kalamata olives: any other type of pitted olive

Balsamic-Fig Pistachio Cheese

YIELD: ABOUT 1 CUP

This unique, sweet cheese will have everyone talking. Despite the brevity of the ingredient list, the final product presents a host of complex flavor interactions that will delight any adventurous palate. (See photo, page 80.)

1/4 cup dried figs, finely chopped

4 teaspoons good-quality balsamic vinegar

4 teaspoons agave nectar

1 batch Basic Nut Cheese (page 82), made with pistachios

In a small bowl, stir together the figs, vinegar, and agave. Spoon the cheese onto a plate and spread into a thick circle (you can use a ring mold if you like), then top with the fig mixture. Serve immediately or refrigerate until the cheese is firm.

Per 2 tablespoon serving: 109 calories, 7.4g fat, 1g sat, 9g carbs, 2g fiber, 3.6g protein

SUBSTITUTIONS

- Figs: golden raisins
- Agave nectar: coconut nectar or any other liquid sweetener

Christmas Cheese Ball

YIELD: ABOUT 1 1/2 CUPS

This cheese is based on my mom's Christmas cheese ball recipe, which she learned from a friend many years ago. When I first heard what was in it, I was afraid to try it—I mean, who combines cream cheese with pineapple, onion, dried fruit, nuts, and...garlic?! Turns out, it's utterly scrumptious. All I had to do was replace the dairy cream cheese with homemade soft cashew cheese, and boom—the perfect party dish and conversation piece, raw-style.

1 batch Basic Nut Cheese (page 82), made with cashews
1/4 cup finely chopped fresh pineapple
2 tablespoons chopped dried cranberries
2 tablespoons finely chopped pecans
2 tablespoons minced green onion
1/4 teaspoon garlic powder

Combine all ingredients in a medium bowl and stir well to combine. Form into a round ball shape on a plate; serve immediately or refrigerate until firm.

Per 2 tablespoon serving: 88 calories, 7.7g fat (1g sat), 4.6g carbs, 1g fiber, 1.7g protein

SUBSTITUTIONS

- Cranberries: raisins
- Pecans: walnuts

Nacho Cheese Sauce

YIELD: ABOUT 2 CUPS `‹30›`

The uses for this sauce are limitless. Dip Zesty Corn Tortilla Chips (page 78) in a big bowlful, use it to coat Cheesy Chili Kale Chips (page 99), try it on Fiesta Taco Roll-Ups (page 162), drizzle it on Taco Salad Supreme (page 128), or just eat it by the spoonful! (You didn't hear that from me...)

1/2 cup cashews, soaked for 2 to 4 hours and drained
1/4 cup hempseeds
1/4 cup nutritional yeast
1 small red bell pepper, seeded and chopped
1 small clove garlic, peeled
2 tablespoons lemon juice
2 tablespoons filtered water
1 1/2 teaspoons chili powder
1/4 teaspoon ground cumin
1/4 teaspoon sea salt
1/8 teaspoon cayenne pepper (optional)

RAW QUESO DIP

For a great raw queso dip, gently warm a bowl of this sauce in the dehydrator or on the stove in a saucepan over low heat.

Combine all ingredients in a high-speed blender and blend until smooth.

Per 1/4 cup serving: 90 calories, 6.3g fat (1g sat), 5g carbs, 1g fiber, 4.4g protein

SUBSTITUTIONS

- Cashews: macadamia nuts
- Hempseeds: sunflower seeds
- Red bell pepper: 1 medium ripe tomato, cored, seeded, and chopped

Garlicky Guacamole

YIELD: ABOUT 1 CUP   ‹30

I love the bite of fresh garlic, but if you're not such a fan, you can replace it with a pinch of garlic powder. I also like to doctor up my guac with plenty of add-ins like onion, tomato, and cilantro, but you can easily leave those out if you prefer.

  2 ripe Hass avocados, pitted, peeled, and chopped
  1 small clove garlic, peeled and minced
  2 tablespoons minced red onion
  2 tablespoons minced tomato
  2 tablespoons minced fresh cilantro
  2 teaspoons lime juice
  1/4 teaspoon ground cumin
  1/4 teaspoon sea salt

Combine all ingredients in a small bowl and use a fork to crush the avocado and stir the mixture together.

Per 2 tablespoon serving: 88 calories, 6.8g fat (1g sat), 7.4g carbs, 4g fiber, 1.3g protein

SUBSTITUTIONS

- Fresh garlic: pinch of garlic powder
- Tomato: red bell pepper
- Lime juice: lemon juice

Garden Fresh Salsa

YIELD: ABOUT 1 1/2 CUPS   `LF` `‹30`

This bright, fresh, pico de gallo-esque salsa makes a great adjunct to any Mexican dish. Use in-season heirloom tomatoes for best results.

4 large ripe tomatoes, cored, seeded, and diced
1/2 small yellow or red bell pepper, seeded and diced
1 small jalapeño or Serrano pepper, seeded and minced (optional)
1/4 cup minced red onion
1/4 cup minced fresh cilantro
1 teaspoon lime juice
1 teaspoon olive oil
1/4 teaspoon sea salt

Combine all ingredients in a medium bowl or container. Refrigerate for at least 30 minutes, or until ready to serve.

Per 1/4 cup serving: 26 calories, .9g fat (trace sat), 4.2g carbs, 1g fiber, .9g protein

VARIATION

Add 1/4 to 1/2 cup diced fresh mango or pineapple for a fruity twist.

Mango Chutney

YIELD: ABOUT 1/2 CUP

I love the chunky mango chutney often served alongside meals at Indian restaurants. This raw version is perfect for spooning onto Naansense Bread (page 67) or dolloping on savory Indian Tartlets (page 146).

1 large ripe mango, peeled, seeded, and chopped
1 tablespoon agave nectar
1 teaspoon lemon juice
1/8 teaspoon cayenne pepper (optional)

Combine the mango, agave, lemon juice, and cayenne pepper, if using, in a food processor and pulse until chunky and combined.

Per 2 tablespoon serving: 49 calories, .2g fat (trace sat), 13g carbs, 1g fiber, .3g protein

SUBSTITUTIONS

- Agave nectar: coconut nectar or any other liquid sweetener
- Lemon juice: lime juice

Basil-Parsley Pesto

YIELD: ABOUT 1 CUP

I adore pesto, but fresh basil can be so expensive that I like to "cut" my pesto with parsley. Pistachios are also a slightly cheaper, yet still somewhat "fancy," alternative to the traditional pine nuts. Leftover pesto can be frozen and enjoyed throughout the winter months when fresh herbs are not available.

1/3 cup dry pistachios

1 small clove garlic, peeled

2 tablespoons nutritional yeast

3/4 teaspoon sea salt

1 bunch fresh basil, stems removed (about 1 cup)

1 bunch fresh flat-leaf parsley, stems removed (1 to 1 1/2 cups)

1/2 teaspoon lemon juice

2 tablespoons olive oil

2 to 3 tablespoons filtered water

Combine the pistachios, garlic, yeast, and salt in a food processor and pulse into coarse crumbs. Add the basil, parsley, and lemon juice and pulse until finely chopped, stopping to scrape down the sides if necessary. Add the oil, a tablespoon at a time, pulsing to combine in between each addition. Add water, a tablespoon at a time, pulsing to combine, until desired consistency is reached.

Per 2 tablespoon serving: 68 calories, 6g fat (1g sat), 2.3g carbs, 1g fiber, 2.1g protein

SUBSTITUTIONS

- Pistachios: walnuts or pine nuts
- Parsley: 1 cup packed fresh spinach

Almond Butter

YIELD: ABOUT 3/4 CUP   ‹30›

Organic raw almond butter is expensive, so I make my own from soaked-and-dehydrated raw almonds, although you can use any kind of dry almonds. The recipe is simple to make, but it does require patience—expect it to take about 15 minutes for the almonds to form a smooth, creamy butter. Use this in any recipe calling for almond butter.

1 1/2 cups dry almonds

Place the almonds into a food processor and pulse into small crumbs. Turn the machine on and let it run for about 12 to 15 minutes, stopping frequently to scrape down the sides of the bowl with a spatula. The almond butter is ready when the nuts have released their oils and the butter is completely smooth and creamy. Transfer to a small container and store in the fridge.

Per tablespoon: 104 calories, 9.1g fat (1g sat), 3.5g carbs, 2g fiber, 3.8g protein

SUBSTITUTIONS

- Almonds: dry cashews, macadamia nuts, hazelnuts, or any other nut

Coconut Butter

YIELD: ABOUT 3/4 CUP ‹30›

Like the almond butter recipe above, a little patience is needed to achieve the proper silky texture for homemade coconut butter. The results are well worth it, though, and at a fraction of the price of store-bought.

2 cups unsweetened shredded coconut

Place the coconut into a food processor, turn the machine on, and let it run for about 12 to 15 minutes, stopping frequently to scrape down the sides of the bowl with a spatula. The coconut butter is ready when it becomes completely smooth and creamy. Transfer to a small container and store in the fridge.

Per tablespoon: 100 calories, 9.7g fat (8g sat), 3.6g carbs, 2.5g fiber, 1g protein

Chocolate Silk Ganache

YIELD: ABOUT 1 1/4 CUPS ‹30›

When freshly made, this thin, drizzly syrup makes an amazing topping for any dessert. When chilled, it morphs into a thick, heavy frosting perfect for cookies, blondies, or brownies.

3/4 cup cacao powder
3/4 cup agave nectar
1/3 cup melted coconut oil
1/2 teaspoon vanilla extract
1/4 teaspoon sea salt

Combine all ingredients in a high-speed blender. Blend on the lowest setting for a few seconds, until the cacao powder is fully incorporated, then blend on high until smooth.

Per tablespoon: 74 calories, 4g fat (3g sat), 11.2g carbs, 1.5g fiber, .6g protein

SUBSTITUTIONS

- Cacao powder: unsweetened cocoa powder or carob powder
- Agave nectar: maple syrup, coconut nectar, or any other liquid sweetener
- Vanilla: hazelnut extract or 2 teaspoons hazelnut liqueur

Vanilla Bean Crème

YIELD: ABOUT 2 CUPS ‹30›

In our house, Matt's the resident chocoholic, while I'm partial to vanilla-flavored sweets. I could eat a whole bowl of this luscious, vanilla-flecked cashew cream. Pour it over just about anything in the Desserts chapter, and you'll be one happy camper.

1 cup cashews, soaked for 2 to 4 hours and drained
1/4 cup Coconut Butter (page 92)
1/4 cup agave nectar
1/4 cup filtered water
Seeds from 1 vanilla bean
1 teaspoon lemon juice
Pinch of sea salt

Combine all ingredients in a high-speed blender and blend until smooth. Add additional water, a tablespoon at a time, if needed to blend.

Per 2 tablespoon serving: 90 calories, 6.1g fat (3g sat), 7.7g carbs, 1g fiber, 1.9g protein

SUBSTITUTIONS

- Agave nectar: coconut nectar or any other liquid sweetener
- Coconut Butter: 2 tablespoons melted coconut oil
- Vanilla bean: 1 tablespoon vanilla extract

Strawberry Coulis

YIELD: ABOUT 1 CUP **LF** **‹30**

Fresh organic strawberries need little more than a touch of agave and lemon juice to make a coulis (a puréed fruit sauce) fit for a king. I like to put it in an indulgent Breakfast Banana Split (page 48) or on any of the ice creams in the Desserts chapter.

1 1/2 cups fresh or thawed frozen strawberries
2 tablespoons agave nectar
1 teaspoon lemon juice
Pinch of sea salt

Combine all ingredients in a high-speed blender and blend until smooth. Strain through a fine mesh sieve, if desired.

Per 2 tablespoon serving: 23 calories, .1g fat (trace sat), 6g carbs, 1g fiber, .2g protein

SUBSTITUTIONS

- Agave nectar: coconut nectar or any other liquid sweetener

Espresso Reduction

YIELD: ABOUT 1/2 CUP `LF` `CO` `<30`

If you're a coffee drinker, you'll love this rich (yet fat-free!) syrup. It goes especially well on Cinnamon Crumble Coffee Cakes (page 207).

1/2 cup cold brewed espresso (or very strong coffee)
1/2 cup maple syrup
Pinch of sea salt

Whisk all ingredients together in a small bowl. Dehydrate overnight or simmer on the stovetop over medium-low heat for about an hour, until reduced by about half.

Per tablespoon: 53 calories, trace fat (trace sat), 13.5g carbs, trace fiber, trace protein

SUBSTITUTIONS

- Maple syrup: agave nectar, coconut nectar, or any other liquid sweetener

Raspberry Jam

YIELD: ABOUT 1 CUP `LF` `<30`

I like seedy berries, so I never strain my homemade jams. Whether you strain this mixture or not, the end result is a tart, thick spread ready to be spooned over Buckwheat-Oat Biscuits (page 74), Classic Vanilla Bean Ice Cream (page 219), or anything else you please.

1 1/2 cups fresh or thawed frozen raspberries
6 pitted dates
1 teaspoon lemon juice
Pinch of sea salt

Combine all ingredients in a high-speed blender and blend until smooth. Strain through a fine mesh sieve, if desired.

Per 2 tablespoon serving: 29 calories, .1g fat (trace sat), 7.5g carbs, 2g fiber, .4g protein

SUBSTITUTIONS

- Raspberries: blackberries or blueberries
- Dates: golden raisins or dried figs

❧ Kale Chips

This may sound like pure blasphemy coming from a raw foodie, but I never liked the taste and texture of most greens. Over the years, I've found numerous ways to sneak them into my diet (such as in juices and smoothies), but the "discovery" of kale chips was a true revelation for me. With kale chips, you can make kale taste like whatever you want. The leaves get crunchy and crisp, like potato chips, and they're packed with powerful plant-based protein. You can even make dessert-y flavors with them! The almighty kale chip may change the way you look at leafy greens, too.

In addition to their awesome taste and addictive crunch, kale chips are one of my favorite ways to increase my intake of greens. Since kale is packed with powerful antioxidants, calcium, and vitamins A, C, and K (plus fiber, omega-3 fatty acids, potassium, and more), that's a beautiful thing. Most of these recipes also provide generous doses of protein, thanks to the nutty coatings. I like to use curly kale to make chips, since it so nicely cradles creamy coatings in all its nooks and crannies, but you can experiment with lacinato (or "dinosaur") kale if you want.

(clockwise from left) Hummus Kale Chips (page 100), Naked Kale Chips (page 98), Cheesy Chili Kale Chips (page 99)

Naked Kale Chips

YIELD: 4 SERVINGS　　

These delicate, shatteringly crisp chips allow you to pop cup after cup of dark leafy greens like it ain't no thang. (See photo, page 96.)

    1 bunch kale, tough stems removed, roughly chopped (6 to 8 cups)
    1 tablespoon olive oil
    1 teaspoon lemon juice
    1/4 teaspoon sea salt

In a large bowl, combine all ingredients. Use your hands to massage the kale until it's softened and evenly coated with oil.

Make It Raw: Arrange the kale in a single layer on a Teflex-lined dehydrator tray. Dehydrate for 8 hours or overnight, until crisp.

Make It Baked: Preheat the oven to 300°F. Grease a baking sheet with coconut oil and arrange the kale on it in a single layer. Bake for about 15 minutes, then remove from the oven and carefully flip the kale chips over. Bake 5 to 10 more minutes, watching to make sure the kale doesn't burn. Remove from the oven and cool completely.

Per serving: 80 calories, 4.1g fat (1g sat), 10.1g carbs, 2g fiber, 3.3g protein

Smokin' Hot Kale Chips

YIELD: 4 SERVINGS　　

Watch out! These chips aren't for the faint of heart. Reduce the amount of chipotle if you're sensitive to heat; otherwise, be ready to have your face melted off! (Not literally.)

    2/3 cup cashews, soaked for 2 to 4 hours and drained
    2 to 3 chipotle chiles in adobo, drained, seeds removed
    2 tablespoons lemon juice
    2 tablespoons filtered water
    1 tablespoon nutritional yeast
    1/2 teaspoon sea salt
    1 bunch kale, tough stems removed, roughly chopped (6 to 8 cups)

Combine all ingredients except the kale in a high-speed blender and blend until smooth, adding a splash of water if needed to blend.

In a large bowl, combine the kale and the cashew sauce. Use your hands to massage the sauce all over the kale, making sure it's coated completely.

Make It Raw: Arrange the kale in a single layer on a Teflex-lined dehydrator tray. Dehydrate for 8 hours or overnight, until crisp.

Make It Baked: Preheat the oven to 300°F. Grease a baking sheet with coconut oil and arrange the kale on it in a single layer. Bake for about 15 minutes, then remove the pan from the oven and carefully flip the kale chips over. Bake 5 to 10 more minutes, watching to make sure the kale doesn't burn. Remove from the oven and cool completely.

Per serving: 195 calories, 11.3g fat (2g sat), 19.7g carbs, 3g fiber, 8.4g protein

SUBSTITUTIONS

- Cashews: macadamia nuts
- Chipotles: fresh jalapeños, seeded and chopped, or 1 tablespoon chili powder plus 1/2 teaspoon cayenne pepper

Cheesy Chili Kale Chips

YIELD: 4 SERVINGS   CO

These beauties give you crunchy chips and cheesy dip all in one package! (See photo, page 96.)

    1 bunch kale, tough stems removed, roughly chopped (6 to 8 cups)
    1 1/2 cups Nacho Cheese Sauce (page 87)

In a large bowl, combine the kale and the cheese sauce. Use your hands to massage the sauce all over the kale, making sure it's coated completely.

Make It Raw: Arrange the kale in a single layer on a Teflex-lined dehydrator tray. Dehydrate for 8 hours or overnight, until crisp.

Make It Baked: Preheat the oven to 300°F. Grease a baking sheet with coconut oil. Arrange the kale in a single layer on the baking sheet and bake for 15 minutes. Remove the pan from the oven and carefully flip the kale chips over. Bake 5 to 10 more minutes, watching carefully to make sure it doesn't burn. Remove from the oven and let cool completely.

Per serving: 192 calories, 9.9g fat (2g sat), 17.6g carbs, 4g fiber, 10g protein

Hummus Kale Chips

YIELD: 4 SERVINGS

These chips are a perfect way to use up leftover hummus! (See photo, page 96.)

> 1 cup Cashew-Macadamia Nut Hummus (page 111)
> 1/4 cup filtered water
> 1 bunch kale, tough stems removed, roughly chopped (6 to 8 cups)

In a large bowl, stir together the hummus and water until smooth, then add the kale. Use your hands to massage the mixture all over the kale, making sure it's coated completely.

Make It Raw: Arrange the kale in a single layer on a Teflex-lined dehydrator tray. Dehydrate for 8 hours or overnight, until crisp.

Make It Baked: Preheat the oven to 300°F. Grease a baking sheet with coconut oil. Arrange the kale in a single layer on the baking sheet and bake for 15 minutes. Remove from the oven and carefully flip the kale chips over. Bake 5 to 10 more minutes, watching carefully to make sure it doesn't burn. Remove from the oven and let cool completely.

Per serving: 243 calories, 18.2g fat (3g sat), 17.6g carbs, 4g fiber, 7.8g protein

Sour Cream and Onion Kale Chips

YIELD: 4 SERVINGS

If you like the tangy taste of sour cream and onion potato chips, you'll adore these.

> 2/3 cup cashews, soaked for 2 to 4 hours and drained
> 1/2 small shallot, peeled
> 2 tablespoons lemon juice
> 2 tablespoons filtered water
> 1 teaspoon agave nectar
> 1/2 teaspoon apple cider vinegar
> 1/2 teaspoon sea salt
> 1 bunch kale, tough stems removed, roughly chopped (6 to 8 cups)

Combine all ingredients except the kale in a high-speed blender and blend until smooth, adding a splash of water if needed to blend.

In a large bowl, combine the kale and the cashew sauce. Use your hands to massage the sauce all over the kale, making sure it's coated completely.

Make It Raw: Arrange the kale in a single layer on a Teflex-lined dehydrator tray. Dehydrate for 8 hours or overnight, until crisp.

Make It Baked: Preheat the oven to 300°F. Grease a baking sheet with coconut oil and arrange the kale on it in a single layer. Bake for about 15 minutes. Remove from the oven and carefully flip the kale chips over. Bake for 5 to 10 more minutes, watching carefully to make sure the kale doesn't burn, then remove from the oven and let cool completely.

Per serving: 190 calories, 11.1g fat (2g sat), 19.8g carbs, 3g fiber, 7.7g protein

SUBSTITUTIONS

- Shallot: 2 tablespoons chopped red onion
- Agave nectar: coconut nectar or any other liquid sweetener
- Apple cider vinegar: coconut vinegar

Curried Kale Chips

YIELD: 4 SERVINGS

Me and curry, I can't get enough. These piquant chips have all the flavors of my favorite Indian dishes.

1/3 cup cashews, soaked for 2 to 4 hours and drained
1/4 cup hempseeds
1/4 cup lemon juice
1/2 large red bell pepper, seeded and chopped
1 tablespoon nutritional yeast
1 tablespoon good-quality curry powder
1 teaspoon chopped fresh ginger
1 clove garlic, peeled
1/2 teaspoon sea salt
1/8 teaspoon cayenne pepper (optional)
1 bunch kale, tough stems removed, roughly chopped (6 to 8 cups)

Combine all ingredients except the kale in a high-speed blender and blend until smooth, adding a splash of water if needed to blend.

In a large bowl, combine the kale and the curry sauce. Use your hands to massage the sauce all over the kale, making sure it's coated completely.

Make It Raw: Arrange the kale in a single layer on a Teflex-lined dehydrator tray. Dehydrate 8 to 10 hours or overnight, until crisp.

Make It Baked: Preheat the oven to 300°F and grease a baking sheet with coconut oil. Arrange the kale in a single layer on the baking sheet and bake for about 15 minutes. Remove the pan from the oven and use a fork or spatula to carefully flip the kale chips over (it's ok if you miss a few). Bake for 5 to 10 more minutes, watching carefully to make sure the kale doesn't burn, then remove from the oven and let cool completely.

Per serving: 190 calories, 10.7g fat (1g sat), 17.9g carbs, 4g fiber, 10g protein

SUBSTITUTIONS:

- Hempseeds: sunflower seeds
- Red bell pepper: 1 medium ripe tomato, cored, seeded, and chopped
- Fresh ginger: 1/2 teaspoon ground ginger

Pizza Kale Chips

YIELD: 4 SERVINGS

If you're at all unsure about the gustatory merits of kale chips, try this recipe first. You'll be shocked at how outrageously fantastic these pizza-flavored crunchers are. (See photo, page 105.)

1/4 cup sunflower seeds, soaked for 2 to 4 hours and drained
1/4 cup hempseeds
1/4 cup nutritional yeast
1/4 cup sundried tomatoes, soaked for 30 minutes and drained
1/2 large red bell pepper, seeded and chopped
1 clove garlic, peeled
2 tablespoons lemon juice
2 tablespoons filtered water
1/2 teaspoon dried oregano
1/2 teaspoon fennel seeds
1/2 teaspoon sea salt
1/4 teaspoon crushed red pepper (optional)
1 bunch kale, tough stems removed, roughly chopped (6 to 8 cups)

Combine all ingredients except the kale in a high-speed blender and blend until smooth, adding a splash of water if needed to blend.

In a large bowl, combine the kale and the pizza sauce. Use your hands to massage the sauce all over the kale, making sure it's coated completely.

Make It Raw: Arrange the kale in a single layer on a Teflex-lined dehydrator tray. Dehydrate for 8 hours or overnight, until crisp.

Make It Baked: Preheat the oven to 300°F and grease a baking sheet with coconut oil. Arrange the kale in a single layer on the baking sheet and bake for about 15 minutes. Remove the pan from the oven and use a fork or spatula to carefully flip the kale chips over (it's ok if you miss a few). Bake for 5 to 10 more minutes, watching carefully to make sure the kale doesn't burn, then remove from the oven and let cool completely.

Per serving: 188 calories, 10g fat (1g sat), 17.5g carbs, 5g fiber, 11.3g protein

SUBSTITUTIONS:

- Hempseeds: additional sunflower seeds or cashews
- Red bell pepper: 1 medium ripe tomato, cored, seeded, and chopped

KALE CHIPS: RAW OR COOKED?

Like many of the recipes in this book, you have the choice of making the kale chips raw or cooked. If you choose to bake these recipes in a conventional oven, please keep a very close eye on your chips, as they can go from crisp to burnt in the blink of an eye. You may want to experiment with a small test batch of chips to see how your oven treats them, and find out if you need to alter the baking time at all.

Chocolate Kale Chips

YIELD: 6 SERVINGS   `CO`

And now, we move on to the sweet flavors. Don't worry—"dessert kale" sounded insane to me at first, too. These dark chocolate kale chips were love at first bite for me, and I'm certain they will be for you, too. They're so sinfully delectable in all their cocoa-laden glory, you'll completely forget you're eating a serving of vegetables at the same time.

2/3 cup cashews, soaked for 2 to 4 hours and drained
1/2 cup maple syrup
1/3 cup cacao powder
1/2 teaspoon vanilla extract
Pinch of sea salt
1 bunch kale, tough stems removed, roughly chopped (6 to 8 cups)

Combine all ingredients except the kale in a high-speed blender and blend until smooth, adding a splash of water if needed to blend.

In a large bowl, combine the kale and the chocolate sauce. Use your hands to massage the sauce all over the kale, making sure it's coated completely.

Make It Raw: Arrange the kale in a single layer on a Teflex-lined dehydrator tray. Dehydrate 8 to 10 hours or overnight, until dry.

Make It Baked: Preheat the oven to 300°F and grease a baking sheet with coconut oil. Arrange the kale in a single layer on the baking sheet and bake for about 15 minutes. Remove the pan from the oven and use a fork or spatula to carefully flip the kale chips over (it's ok if you miss a few). Bake for about 10 more minutes, watching carefully to make sure the kale doesn't burn, then remove from the oven and let cool completely.

Per serving: 201 calories, 8g fat (2g sat), 31.8g carbs, 3g fiber, 6g protein

SUBSTITUTIONS

- Maple syrup: agave nectar, coconut nectar, or any other liquid sweetener (chips will be less crisp)
- Cacao powder: unsweetened cocoa powder or carob powder

VARIATION

Replace (half or all) the cashews with walnuts or pecans to make Nutty Chocolate Kale Chips.

Chocolate Kale Chips (left), Pizza Kale Chips (page 102)

Coconut-Vanilla Kale Chips

YIELD: 6 SERVINGS   `CO`

Once you try these vanilla-kissed chippers, you'll be hooked.

- 2/3 cup cashews, soaked for 2 to 4 hours and drained
- 1/4 cup maple syrup
- 1/4 cup agave nectar
- 1/3 cup unsweetened shredded coconut
- 1 teaspoon vanilla extract
- Pinch of sea salt
- 1 bunch kale, tough stems removed, roughly chopped (6 to 8 cups)

Combine all ingredients except the kale in a high-speed blender and blend until smooth, adding a splash of water if needed to blend.

In a large bowl, combine the kale and the cashew-coconut sauce. Use your hands to massage the sauce all over the kale, making sure it's coated completely.

Make It Raw: Arrange the kale in a single layer on a Teflex-lined dehydrator tray. Dehydrate 8 to 10 hours or overnight, until dry.

Make It Baked: Preheat the oven to 300°F and grease a baking sheet with coconut oil. Arrange the kale in a single layer on the baking sheet and bake for about 15 minutes. Remove the pan from the oven and use a fork or spatula to carefully flip the kale chips over (it's ok if you miss a few). Bake for 5 to 10 more minutes, watching carefully to make sure the kale doesn't burn, then remove from the oven and let cool completely.

Per serving: 213 calories, 8.9g fat (3g sat), 31.8g carbs, 3g fiber, 5.2g protein

SUBSTITUTIONS

- Maple syrup: additional agave nectar, coconut nectar, or any other liquid sweetener (chips will be less crisp)
- Agave nectar: additional maple syrup, coconut nectar, or any other liquid sweetener
- Shredded coconut: 1/4 cup Coconut Butter (page 92)

Maple-Pecan Kale Chips

YIELD: 6 SERVINGS　`CO`

The crunch of these chips combined with the warm, nutty flavor makes me think of stomping on crisp fallen leaves in cool autumn weather. Pure heaven.

 3/4 cup pecans, soaked 2 to 4 hours and drained
 1/2 cup maple syrup
 1/2 teaspoon vanilla extract
 1/4 teaspoon ground cinnamon
 Pinch of sea salt
 1 bunch kale, tough stems removed, roughly chopped (about 6 to 8 cups)

Combine all ingredients except the kale in a high-speed blender and blend until smooth, adding a splash of water if needed to blend.

In a large bowl, combine the kale and the maple-pecan sauce. Use your hands to massage the sauce all over the kale, making sure it's coated completely.

Make It Raw: Arrange the kale in a single layer on a Teflex-lined dehydrator tray. Dehydrate 8 to 10 hours or overnight, until dry.

Make It Baked: Preheat the oven to 300°F and grease a baking sheet with coconut oil. Arrange the kale in a single layer on the baking sheet and bake for about 15 minutes. Remove the pan from the oven and use a fork or spatula to carefully flip the kale chips over (it's ok if you miss a few). Bake for 5 to 10 more minutes, watching carefully to make sure the kale doesn't burn, then remove from the oven and let cool completely.

Per serving: 198 calories, 10.2g fat (1g sat), 26.6g carbs, 3g fiber, 3.5g protein

SUBSTITUTIONS

- Maple syrup: agave nectar, coconut nectar, or other liquid sweetener (chips will be less crisp)

∼ Hummus

To me, hummus is the world's most perfect food: quick to make, creamy and rich, smooth and savory, and as spicy or mild as you want it. I love the classic chickpea variety, but raw hummus is also an excitingly bare canvas just begging to be painted with any combination of flavors and spices you can dream up.

Hummus is, to me, what salad is to other raw foodists: a near-daily staple!

In this chapter, I offer you three base hummus recipes: one using chickpeas, one with zucchini, and one made with nuts. The remaining recipes utilize your choice of base plus a plethora of mouthwatering seasonings to create some of the most delicious and eclectic hummus varieties you'll ever eat. I excluded nutritional calculations for the flavored variations simply because they're dependent on which base hummus recipe you choose to use.

Zucchini Hummus (page 110)

Classic Chickpea Hummus

YIELD: ABOUT 2 CUPS `CO` `‹30`

Legumes may not be raw, but they're still mega-healthy! You can experiment with using sprouted chickpeas if you like, but I prefer them cooked.

> 1 1/2 cups cooked or 1 (15-ounce) can chickpeas, rinsed and drained
> 1/4 cup tahini
> 2 tablespoons lemon juice
> 1 tablespoon olive oil
> 1 small clove garlic, peeled
> 1/2 teaspoon sea salt
> 1/8 teaspoon ground cumin

Combine all ingredients in a high-speed blender or food processor and blend until smooth, adding water a tablespoon at a time if needed to thin. Transfer to a small bowl or container and refrigerate for at least one hour before serving.

Per 1/4 cup serving: 115 calories, 6.2g fat (1g sat), 12.2g carbs, 3g fiber, 3.5g protein

Zucchini Hummus

YIELD: ABOUT 2 1/4 CUPS `‹30`

In this hummus, the lighter of my two raw base recipes, the mild taste of the zucchini all but disappears behind the assertive sesame seed flavor. I include a tiny bit of sweetener to cut the bitterness of the tahini. (See photo, page 108.)

> 1 large or 1 1/2 medium zucchini, peeled and chopped (2 1/2 to 3 cups)
> 1/2 cup tahini
> 2 tablespoons lemon juice
> 1 small clove garlic, peeled
> 1/2 teaspoon agave nectar
> 1/2 teaspoon sea salt
> 1/4 teaspoon ground cumin

Combine all ingredients in a high-speed blender or food processor and blend until smooth.

Taste for seasoning, adding an additional 1/8 to 1/4 teaspoon salt if desired. Transfer to a small bowl or container and refrigerate for at least one hour before serving.

Per 1/4 cup serving: 85 calories, 6.5g fat (1g sat), 5.4g carbs, 2g fiber, 2.9g protein

Cashew-Macadamia Nut Hummus

YIELD: ABOUT 2 CUPS

This nut-based raw hummus is thicker and richer than the zucchini version. It's also my personal favorite!

3/4 cup cashews, soaked 2 to 4 hours and drained
1/2 cup macadamia nuts, soaked 2 to 4 hours and drained
1/4 cup tahini
2 tablespoons lemon juice
1 tablespoon olive oil
1/2 teaspoon sea salt
1/2 small clove garlic, peeled
3/4 to 1 cup filtered water, as needed to thin

Combine all ingredients, including 3/4 cup water, in a high-speed blender and blend until smooth. Add additional water, 2 tablespoons at a time, as needed to thin. Transfer to a small bowl or container and refrigerate for at least one hour before serving.

Per 1/4 cup serving: 193 calories, 17.5g fat (3g sat), 7.6g carbs, 2g fiber, 4.5g protein

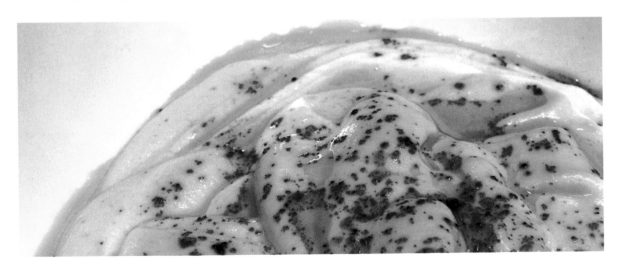

Note: Nutritional calculations for the flavored hummus recipes have not been included as the data depends upon which base hummus recipe is used. See recipes above for the data.

Lemon Garlic Hummus

YIELD: ABOUT 2 1/4 CUPS　‹30›

This bright, sunny-tasting hummus is also a garlic lover's dream.

> 2 cups Base Hummus of choice
> 2 tablespoons lemon juice
> 2 teaspoons lemon zest
> 1 small clove garlic, peeled
> Sea salt to taste

Combine the hummus, lemon juice, zest, and garlic in a high-speed blender and blend until smooth. Add salt to taste. Transfer to a small bowl or container and refrigerate for at least one hour before serving.

Kalamata Olive Hummus

YIELD: ABOUT 2 1/2 CUPS　‹30›

Kalamatas really are where it's at, if you ask me, but there's no reason you can't use another type of olive instead. You can make this hummus as chunky or as smooth as you want.

> 2 cups Base Hummus of choice
> 1/2 cup pitted Kalamata olives
> 1/4 teaspoon dried oregano

Combine all ingredients in a food processor and pulse together until desired consistency is achieved. Transfer to a small bowl or container and refrigerate for at least one hour before serving.

Red Pepper Hummus

YIELD: ABOUT 2 1/2 CUPS

Roasted red pepper is a classic and much-loved flavor for hummus. If you don't care to dehy-drate the bell pepper, you can simply leave it raw; just expect a thinner consistency. Use your choice of sweet, smoked, or hot paprika.

1 large red bell pepper, seeded and roughly chopped
1 teaspoon olive oil
2 cups Base Hummus of choice
2 teaspoons paprika, any kind
Sea salt to taste

Rub the red pepper pieces with the olive oil and place on a Teflex-lined dehydrator tray. Dehydrate for about 4 hours, until the pieces are softened and shrunken in size.

Combine the softened red pepper, hummus, and paprika in a high-speed blender and blend until smooth. Add salt to taste. Transfer to a small bowl or container and refrigerate for at least one hour before serving.

COOKED VARIATION

Use a jarred or homemade roasted red pepper instead of dehydrating one.

Marinated Mushroom Hummus

YIELD: ABOUT 2 1/2 CUPS

This earthy spread is full of "umami." Spoon it on top of Mushroom-Nut Burgers (page 144) if you're a serious 'shroom fanatic.

2 cups Base Hummus of choice
1/2 cup + 2 tablespoons Simple Seasoned Mushrooms (page 174), divided
Sea salt to taste

Combine the hummus and 1/2 cup of the mushrooms in a food processor and pulse until desired consistency is achieved. Add salt to taste. Transfer to a small bowl or container and refrigerate for at least one hour before serving.

Just before serving, roughly chop the remaining 2 tablespoons of mushrooms and sprinkle them on top of the hummus.

Ethiopian-Spiced Hummus

YIELD: ABOUT 2 1/4 CUPS 〈30〉

Berbere is a fragrant, robust Ethiopian spice mixture I think of as the love child of chili powder and curry powder, with a unique African flair. There's truly no substitute for it and is worth the effort to seek it out (available online). You'll have no trouble finding myriad uses for it...that is, if you can stop yourself from making batch after batch of this hummus!

2 cups Base Hummus of choice
2 tablespoons berbere powder
2 teaspoons lemon or lime juice
1 teaspoon chopped fresh ginger or 1/2 teaspoon ground ginger
1/2 teaspoon ground cardamom
1/8 teaspoon sea salt
1/8 teaspoon cayenne pepper (optional)

Combine all ingredients in a high-speed blender and blend until smooth. Transfer to a small bowl or container and refrigerate for at least one hour before serving.

Sundried Tomato-Pesto Hummus

YIELD: ABOUT 2 1/2 CUPS

Serve this Italian-inspired hummus with Rosemary-Garlic Bread (page 66) or Mediterranean Herb Crackers (page 76).

2 cups Base Hummus of choice

1/2 cup sundried tomatoes, soaked for 30 minutes and drained

Sea salt to taste

2 tablespoons Basil-Parsley Pesto (page 91)

1 tablespoon olive oil

Combine the hummus and sundried tomatoes in a high-speed blender and blend until smooth. Add salt to taste. Transfer to a small bowl or container and refrigerate for at least one hour.

Just before serving, stir the pesto and oil together in a small bowl. Make a well in the center of the hummus and spoon in the pesto-oil mixture.

Smokin' Hot Hummus

YIELD: ABOUT 2 1/4 CUPS

Some like it hot...and I'm one of 'em. Though I don't normally care for smoky flavors, chipotle is an exception. You could always use a raw jalapeño instead if you wanted. Use your choice of sweet, hot, or smoked paprika.

2 cups Base Hummus of choice

2 to 3 chipotle chiles in adobo, drained, seeds removed

2 teaspoons paprika, any kind

1/2 teaspoon ground coriander

Sea salt to taste

Crushed red pepper, for garnish (optional)

Combine the hummus, chipotle, paprika, and coriander in a high-speed blender and blend until smooth. Add salt to taste. Transfer to a small bowl or container and refrigerate for at least one hour. Sprinkle with crushed red pepper, if desired, before serving.

Italian Herb Hummus

YIELD: ABOUT 2 1/4 CUPS

This herb-packed hummus makes a dreamy dip for Mediterranean Herb Crackers (page 76) or Rosemary-Garlic Bread (page 66).

    2 cups Base Hummus of choice
    1/2 small clove garlic, peeled
    1/2 cup chopped fresh flat-leaf parsley
    10 to 12 large basil leaves, roughly chopped
    1 teaspoon dried oregano
    Sea salt to taste

Combine the hummus and garlic in a food processor and process until smooth. Add the parsley, basil, and oregano and pulse together until desired consistency is achieved. Add salt to taste. Transfer to a small bowl or container and refrigerate for at least one hour before serving.

Curried Indian Hummus

YIELD: ABOUT 2 1/4 CUPS   <30

If you haven't noticed already, you'll know by the end of this book that I'm a little obsessed with Indian flavors. This curry-spiced hummus goes particularly well with Naansense Bread (page 67).

    2 cups Base Hummus of choice
    2 tablespoons good-quality curry powder
    1/2 small clove garlic, peeled
    2 teaspoons minced fresh ginger or 1/2 teaspoon ground ginger
    2 teaspoons cumin seeds or 1 teaspoon ground cumin
    1/2 teaspoon ground coriander
    1/2 teaspoon turmeric
    1/8 teaspoon sea salt
    1/8 teaspoon cayenne pepper (optional)

Combine all ingredients in a high-speed blender and blend until smooth. Transfer to a small bowl or container and refrigerate for at least one hour before serving.

Tex-Mex Hummus

YIELD: ABOUT 2 1/4 CUPS `‹30`

Serve this Southwestern-style hummus with homemade Zesty Corn Tortilla Chips (page 78), or just pop open a bag of good-quality store-bought chips.

2 cups Base Hummus of choice

1/4 cup sundried tomatoes, soaked for 30 minutes and drained

2 teaspoons lime juice

2 teaspoons chili powder

2 teaspoons ground cumin

1 teaspoon ground coriander

1/2 small clove garlic, peeled

1/4 cup chopped fresh cilantro

Sea salt to taste

Combine all ingredients except cilantro and salt in a high-speed blender and blend until smooth. Add cilantro and blend briefly to incorporate. Add salt to taste. Transfer to a small bowl or container and refrigerate for at least one hour before serving.

～ Soups & Salads

Raw soup can be a busy person's best friend. Within moments, you can have a smooth, puréed meal full of fresh vegetables, healthy fats, and lots of flavor. They're a fast, easy, and delicious way to pack tons of vitamins and minerals into a compact package. Embrace summer with a velvety avocado soup or a light bell pepper bisque, or go down the comfort-food route with a rich mushroom cream soup. Get your beta-carotene fix with a carrot- or butternut squash-based blend, or take a walk on the wild side with a sweet watermelon-white wine soup. There's something for every mood and season here.

Although I'm not much of a salad girl myself, I couldn't write a raw cookbook without at least a few salads! You'll find that the salads in this chapter are simple to prepare, yet still full of great flavor. It won't take you long to whip up a massaged kale salad fit for a king, or an Italian-inspired salad with a zippy Catalina-esque dressing. I also often like to use salad as a vehicle for leftovers, as you'll see in the Taco Salad Supreme and the Hummus Amongus Salad, so they're a great way to clean out your fridge.

Kale Tahini Salad (page 130)

Butternut Squash-Chipotle Soup

YIELD: 4 SERVINGS   `CO`   `‹30`

When you're craving warmer flavors in the fall or winter months, turn to this soup for spoonful after spoonful of comfort.

    1/2 small butternut squash, peeled, seeded, and cubed (about 2 cups)
    1 small apple, peeled, cored, and chopped
    1 cup filtered water
    1/2 cup orange juice
    1/4 cup cashews, soaked for 2 to 4 hours and drained
    2 tablespoons olive oil
    1 chipotle chile in adobo, drained, seeds removed
    1 teaspoon ground cumin
    1/2 teaspoon ground cinnamon
    1/2 teaspoon sea salt, or to taste

Combine all ingredients in a high-speed blender and blend until smooth.

Make It Raw: Transfer the soup to a large bowl or container and warm it in the dehydrator for 1 hour before serving. Alternatively, serve the soup at room temperature or chill it in the refrigerator for a few hours before serving.

Make It Cooked: Transfer the soup to a medium saucepan and gently warm it on the stove over low heat.

Per 1 cup serving: 180 calories, 11g fat (2g sat), 20.2g carbs, 3g fiber, 2.7g protein

SUBSTITUTIONS

- Squash: 4 to 5 large carrots
- Apple: pear
- Orange juice: apple juice or 2 to 3 tablespoons lemon juice
- Chipotle: fresh jalapeño, seeded and chopped, or 1 teaspoon chili powder plus 1/8 teaspoon cayenne pepper

Cream of Mushroom Soup

YIELD: 4 SERVINGS   CO

I love a good full-bodied soup such as this when it's chilly outside. Warm it up slightly before serving to boost the comfort food factor.

1 batch Simple Seasoned Mushrooms (page 174), divided
1 cup cashews, soaked for 2 to 4 hours and drained
1 cup filtered water
1 rib celery, chopped
1 small clove garlic, peeled
1/2 medium shallot, peeled
1 tablespoon nutritional yeast
2 teaspoons lemon juice
1 teaspoon white miso
1 teaspoon agave nectar
1/2 teaspoon dried thyme
1/2 teaspoon sea salt, or to taste

Combine all ingredients except 1/4 cup of the Simple Seasoned Mushrooms in a high-speed blender and blend until smooth.

Make It Raw: Transfer the soup to a large bowl or container and warm it in the dehydrator for 1 hour before serving. Alternatively, serve the soup at room temperature or chill it in the refrigerator for a few hours before serving.

Make It Cooked: Transfer the soup to a medium saucepan and gently warm it on the stove over low heat.

Garnish each serving with a tablespoon of the reserved Simple Seasoned Mushrooms.

Per 1 cup serving: 285 calories, 22.5g fat (4g sat), 15.9g carbs, 2g fiber, 9.1g protein

SUBSTITUTIONS

- Shallot: 2 tablespoons chopped red onion
- Agave nectar: coconut nectar or any other liquid sweetener

Curried Carrot-Coconut Soup

YIELD: 4 SERVINGS   `CO`   `‹30`

Spicy curry, sweet carrot, and succulent coconut marry together in this easy soup. It's like food polyamory, in the best way.

8 large carrots, peeled and chopped
1 cup filtered water
1/2 cup chopped young coconut meat
1/2 cup Almond Milk (page 30) (preferably unsweetened)
1 tablespoon good-quality curry powder
2 teaspoons lemon juice
1 teaspoon chopped fresh ginger or 1/2 teaspoon ground dried ginger
1/2 small clove garlic, peeled
1 teaspoon sea salt, or to taste
2 tablespoons melted coconut oil
4 teaspoons unsweetened shredded coconut (optional), for garnish

Combine the carrots, water, coconut meat, almond milk, curry powder, lemon juice, ginger, garlic, and salt in a high-speed blender and blend until smooth. With the machine running, stream in the coconut oil and blend until very smooth.

Make It Raw: Transfer the soup to a large bowl or container and warm it in the dehydrator for 1 hour before serving. Alternatively, serve the soup at room temperature or chill it in the refrigerator for a few hours before serving.

Make It Cooked: Transfer the soup to a medium saucepan and gently warm it on the stove over low heat.

Garnish each serving with 1 teaspoon unsweetened shredded coconut, if desired.

Per 1 cup serving: 148 calories, 11.4g fat (9g sat), 12g carbs, 4g fiber, 1.7g protein

SUBSTITUTIONS

- Coconut meat: 1/4 cup Coconut Butter (page 92) plus 1/4 cup filtered water
- Almond Milk: Coconut Milk (page 31), store-bought refrigerated (not canned) coconut milk, or any other unsweetened nondairy milk
- Coconut oil: olive oil

Chilled Watermelon Soup

YIELD: 4 SERVINGS   `LF` `‹30`

This sweet and simple summertime soup is a treat for adult palates.

2 pounds chopped seedless watermelon
1/4 cup sweet white wine (such as Riesling)
2 tablespoons agave nectar
Pinch of sea salt
1 cup green grapes, halved
1/2 cup golden raisins
Chopped fresh mint, for garnish (optional)

In a high-speed blender, combine the watermelon, wine, agave, and salt, and blend until very smooth. Transfer to a bowl and stir in the raisins and grapes. Chill for at least 2 hours to allow the fruit to macerate. Serve cold, garnished with mint, if desired.

Per serving: 194 calories, 1.1g fat (trace sat), 46g carbs, 3g fiber, 2.3g protein

SUBSTITUTIONS

- Agave nectar: coconut nectar or any other liquid sweetener
- Wine: kombucha, or 3 tablespoons filtered water plus 1 tablespoon lime juice
- Grapes: chopped honeydew melon
- Raisins: dried mulberries

Avocado Cream Soup

YIELD: 4 SERVINGS   `‹30`

This is a cooling, refreshing soup with a Southwestern edge. Be sure to allow an hour or two for the soup to chill before enjoying.

2 ripe Hass avocados, pitted, peeled, and chopped

1/2 cup cashews, soaked for 2 to 4 hours and drained

2 green onions, ends trimmed, chopped

1/2 clove garlic, peeled

1 tablespoon lime juice

3/4 teaspoon sea salt, or to taste

1/2 teaspoon ground cumin

2 1/4 cups filtered water

1 small Roma tomato, cored, seeded, and diced (optional)

Chopped fresh cilantro (optional)

In a high-speed blender, combine the avocados, cashews, green onion, garlic, lime juice, salt, cumin, and water and blend until very smooth. Transfer to a bowl, cover, and refrigerate for 1 to 2 hours (no longer), until chilled. Taste and adjust seasonings, if needed. Garnish with tomatoes and cilantro, if desired.

Per 1 cup serving: 132 calories, 10.6g fat (1g sat), 6.2g carbs, 5g fiber, 5g protein.

SUBSTITUTIONS

- Green onions: 1 tablespoon minced red onion
- Lime juice: lemon juice

Red Pepper-Pistachio Bisque

YIELD: 4 SERVINGS   `CO` `<30`

A creamy, paprika-laced red bell pepper bisque such as this is just begging for a dollop of herby pesto on top, but feel free to serve it plain if you prefer. (See photo, page 127.)

2 medium red bell peppers, seeded and chopped

1/4 cup pistachios, soaked for 2 to 4 hours and drained

1/4 cup cashews, soaked for 2 to 4 hours and drained

1 small shallot, peeled and chopped

1 small jalapeño or Serrano pepper, stemmed and seeded (optional)

1 cup Almond Milk (page 30) (preferably unsweetened)

1 cup filtered water

2 teaspoons sweet paprika

2 teaspoons lemon juice

1 teaspoon sea salt, or to taste

1/2 teaspoon ground cumin

1/4 teaspoon ground cardamom

1 small or 1/2 large ripe Hass avocado, pitted and peeled

4 tablespoons Basil-Parsley Pesto (page 91) (optional)

GOT PAPRIKA?

If you have sweet Hungarian paprika in your cupboard, definitely use it here.

Combine all ingredients except avocado and pesto in a high-speed blender and blend until smooth. Add the avocado and blend again until very smooth.

Make It Raw: Transfer the bisque to a large bowl or container and warm it in the dehydrator for 1 hour before serving. Alternatively, serve the soup at room temperature or chill it in the refrigerator for a few hours before serving.

Make It Cooked: Transfer the bisque to a medium saucepan and gently warm it on the stove over low heat.

To serve, divide the bisque among four shallow bowls. Spoon 1 tablespoon of the pesto in the center of each bowl, if desired.

Per 1 cup serving: 186 calories, 12g fat (1.5g sat), 16.4g carbs, 5g fiber, 5.7g protein

SUBSTITUTIONS

- Pistachios: additional cashews
- Shallot: 1/4 cup chopped red onion
- Almond Milk: Coconut Milk (page 31) or any other unsweetened nondairy milk

Red Pepper Pistachio Bisque (page 125) with Basil-Parsely Pesto (page 91)

Matt's Salad Sprinkle

YIELD: ABOUT 1 CUP

I created this simple sprinkle to add to Matt's salads. It adds flavor, texture, and extra nutrition. Now, he won't eat a salad without it! The cheesy-tasting nutritional yeast delivers protein and B vitamins, the dulse lends a subtly salty taste and a dose of iodine, and the hempseeds add crunch while also contributing omega-3 fatty acids.

1/2 cup nutritional yeast
6 tablespoons hempseeds
1 to 2 tablespoons dulse flakes

Combine all ingredients in a small container with a lid. Cover and shake to combine. Add 1 to 2 tablespoons to any salad for a tasty nutrient boost. Store in the refrigerator.

Per tablespoon: 28 calories, 1.8g fat (trace sat), .9g carbs, trace fiber, 2.1g protein

SUBSTITUTIONS

- Hempseeds: sesame seeds
- Dulse: 1/2 teaspoon sea salt

Taco Salad Supreme

YIELD: 4 SERVINGS   `CO`

Every time I make Fiesta Taco Roll-Ups (page 162), I find myself with plenty of leftovers. I like to toss everything together the next day to make this quick Mexi-salad. Leftover taco "meat" and crumbled Zesty Corn Tortilla Chips (page 78) are a nice touch, too, if you have some on hand. (Photo opposite.)

10 to 12 cups chopped romaine lettuce
1/2 batch Nacho Cheese Sauce (page 87)
1/2 cup fresh or thawed frozen corn kernels
1/2 medium ripe Hass avocado, pitted, peeled, and diced
1/2 batch Garden Fresh Salsa (page 89)
Leftover taco "meat" from Fiesta Taco Roll-Ups (page 162) (optional)
A handful of Zesty Corn Tortilla Chips (page 78) (optional)

In a large bowl, toss the romaine with the Nacho Cheese Sauce until lightly coated. Divide the salad between four serving plates or bowls and top each portion with the corn, avocado, and Garden Fresh Salsa. Crumble and add the leftover taco "meat" and/or a few Zesty Corn Tortilla Chips, if desired.

Per serving (w/o "meat" or chips): 203 calories, 11.6g fat (2g sat), 20.5g carbs, 8g fiber, 9.1g protein

SUBSTITUTIONS

- Romaine: any other leafy green
- Avocado: 1/2 batch Garlicky Guacamole (page 88)
- Garden Fresh Salsa: store-bought salsa

COOKED VARIATION

Include 1/2 to 1 cup cooked black beans, pinto beans, or vegan refried beans in place of the leftover taco "meat."

Taco Salad Supreme (page 128)

Hummus Amongus Salad

YIELD: 4 SERVINGS

This is my favorite clean-out-the-fridge salad! It's a great way to use up the last of a batch of hummus and veggie scraps that may be languishing in the refrigerator.

10 to 12 cups chopped romaine lettuce

2 to 3 cups mixed raw vegetables, such as broccoli or cauliflower florets, sliced red bell
  pepper, halved grape tomatoes, shredded carrots, sliced red onion, etc.

1 cup Zucchini Hummus (page 110)

In a large bowl, toss the romaine and veggies with the hummus until coated. Divide the salad between four serving plates or bowls; serve immediately.

Per serving: 158 calories, 7.1g fat (1g sat), 19.6g carbs, 7g fiber, 7.5g protein*

*These nutritional values are approximate, and will vary slightly depending on the vegetables used.

SUBSTITUTIONS

- Romaine: any other leafy green
- Zucchini Hummus: any other type of hummus (see the Hummus chapter)

Kale-Tahini Salad

YIELD: 4 SERVINGS

This salad pays homage to Russell James, the king of massaged kale salads and the first person to convince me to try one! It's so hearty and filling, it's a meal in itself. Spice-phobes can feel free to omit the chipotle; the creamy tahini dressing is just as divine without it. (See photo, page 118.)

1/2 cup tahini

1/4 cup olive oil

1/4 cup filtered water

2 tablespoons lemon juice

1 chipotle chile in adobo, drained, seeds removed

1 teaspoon agave nectar

1 teaspoon ground cumin

1 teaspoon ground coriander

1 teaspoon sea salt

1 bunch kale, tough stems removed, roughly chopped (6 to 8 cups)

1 large ripe tomato, cored, seeded, and diced

4 teaspoons hempseeds

Combine the tahini, oil, water, lemon juice, chipotle, agave, cumin, coriander, and salt in a high-speed blender and blend until smooth. Place the kale in a large bowl and add the tahini dressing. Use your hands to thoroughly massage the dressing into the kale until it is softened and completely coated.

Divide between four serving plates or bowls and top each portion with the diced tomato and 1 teaspoon hempseeds.

Per serving: 383 calories, 31.8g fat (4g sat), 20.3g carbs, 4g fiber, 10.1g protein

SUBSTITUTIONS

- Chipotle: fresh jalapeño, seeded and chopped, or 1 teaspoon chili powder
- Agave nectar: coconut nectar or any other liquid sweetener
- Tomato: 1 1/2 cups grape or cherry tomatoes, halved
- Hempseeds: sesame seeds

Insalata di Trattoria

YIELD: 4 SERVINGS   ‹30›

A trattoria is a casual Italian eatery, the perfect place for an al fresco lunch and a nice glass of vino. Pop open a bottle of your favorite white wine to sip alongside this salad (making sure to save 1/4 cup of it to make the Chilled Watermelon Soup on page 123!).

For the dressing:

1 large ripe tomato, cored, seeded, and chopped

2 teaspoons lemon juice

1 teaspoon red wine vinegar

1 small pitted date

2 tablespoons olive oil

1/4 teaspoon sea salt

1/8 teaspoon garlic powder

1/8 teaspoon dried oregano

1/8 teaspoon dried basil

1/8 teaspoon black pepper

For the salad:

10 to 12 cups chopped romaine lettuce

2 cups grape or cherry tomatoes, halved

1 cup thinly sliced red onion

Combine all dressing ingredients in a high-speed blender and blend until very smooth. Add 1 to 2 tablespoons of water to help it blend, if necessary.

In a large bowl, toss the romaine, tomatoes, and onion with the dressing until coated. Divide the salad between four serving plates or bowls.

Per serving: 150 calories, 7.8g fat (1g sat), 19.1g carbs, 6g fiber, 5.1g protein

SUBSTITUTIONS

- Romaine: any other leafy green
- Grape tomatoes: 1 large ripe tomato, cored, seeded, and chopped

Greek Taverna Salad

YIELD: 4 SERVINGS

This salad is a typical appetizer you might encounter at a Greek taverna. Not to be confused with "taverns," tavernes (plural of taverna) are lively restaurants found throughout Greece.

For the dressing:
1/4 cup olive oil
2 tablespoons lemon juice
1 teaspoon ground oregano
1 teaspoon sea salt
For the salad:
10 to 12 cups chopped romaine lettuce
1 seedless cucumber, peeled if desired and diced
1 large ripe tomato, cored, seeded, and diced
1 cup thinly sliced red onion
1/2 cup pitted Kalamata olives, roughly chopped
1/2 cup chopped fresh flat-leaf parsley
1/2 cup Basic Nut Cheese (page 82), preferably made with macadamia nuts, crumbled

Whisk all dressing ingredients together in a small bowl.

In a large bowl, combine the romaine, cucumber, tomato, and onion. Add the dressing and toss to coat. Divide the salad between four serving plates or bowls and top each serving with 2 tablespoons each of olives, parsley, and crumbled Basic Nut Cheese.

Per serving: 307 calories, 26.7g fat (4g sat), 16g carbs, 6g fiber, 6.2g protein

SUBSTITUTIONS

- Tomato: 1 1/2 cup grape or cherry tomatoes, halved
- Kalamata olives: any other olive or 1/3 cup rinsed and drained capers
- Basic Nut Cheese: vegan feta cheese or crumbled firm tofu

Spinach Salad with Asian Ginger Vinaigrette

YIELD: 4 SERVINGS   `‹30`

This simple salad provides maximum flavor with minimum effort.

For the dressing:
1/4 cup olive oil
2 tablespoons tamari
1 tablespoon sesame oil
1 tablespoon rice vinegar
1 tablespoon minced fresh ginger
1 teaspoon agave nectar
1/2 teaspoon sea salt
For the salad:
8 cups baby spinach
2 medium carrots, peeled if desired and shredded
1/2 seedless cucumber, peeled if desired and diced
4 teaspoons sesame seeds

Whisk all dressing ingredients together in a small bowl.

In a large bowl, toss the spinach, carrots, and cucumber with the dressing until well-coated. Divide the salad between four serving plates or bowls and top each serving with 1 teaspoon sesame seeds.

Per serving: 194 calories, 18.6g fat (3g sat), 5.2g carbs, 7g fiber, 3.5g protein

SUBSTITUTIONS

- Tamari: soy sauce, nama shoyu, or liquid aminos
- Agave nectar: coconut nectar or any other liquid sweetener
- Sesame seeds: hempseeds

Main Dishes

This chapter contains a smorgasbord of main-meal recipes that run the gamut from international to all-American, from light to indulgent, and from quick-to-prepare to fancier fare. You're sure to find some of your favorite foods in the pages that follow, such as pasta and noodles, burgers and wraps, curries and stir fries, tacos and pizzas, and more—all raw and all ultra-delish! Some of these dishes make great grab-and-go lunches, while others would be right at home at a stylish dinner party—there's something for every occasion here.

Note: Any time a dish has multiple parts or layers—like pasta + sauce, rice + curry, etc.—you'll want to keep the components separate until just before serving, and store them separately as well if you're keeping leftovers (unless otherwise indicated). This way, your dishes will be as fresh and vibrant as possible when you sit down to eat.

(clockwise from bottom center) Fiesta Taco Roll-Ups (page 162), Nacho Cheese Sauce (page 87), taco "meat," Zesty Corn Tortilla Chips (page 78), Garden Fresh Salsa (page 89), and Garlicky Guacamole (page 88)

Spaghetti alla Marinara

YIELD: 4 SERVINGS   `LF` `CO` `‹30`

I wasn't wild on raw marinara sauce until I discovered the magic formula—approximately a 1:1 ratio of sundried tomatoes to fresh, plus a date to balance the tomatoes' acidity. When you taste this full-flavored sauce, I hope you'll become a convert too! For a chunkier sauce, make it in a food processor and use even less water.

For the marinara sauce:

1 cup sundried tomatoes, soaked for 30 minutes and drained

2 medium ripe tomatoes, cored, seeded, and chopped

1 large or 2 small pitted dates

1 small clove garlic, peeled

2 tablespoons nutritional yeast

1 tablespoon olive oil

2 teaspoons dried oregano

1 teaspoon balsamic vinegar

1/2 teaspoon sea salt

1/2 to 3/4 cup filtered water, as needed

For the spaghetti:

4 medium zucchini, peeled if desired, spiralized

Combine all sauce ingredients including 1/2 cup water, in a high-speed blender and blend to combine. Add more water, 2 tablespoons at a time, as needed to help blend smoothly. The sauce should be thick.

In a large bowl, toss the zucchini noodles with the marinara sauce. Serve immediately.

Per serving: 124 calories, 4.4g fat (1g sat), 20g carbs, 6g fiber, 5.7g protein

SUBSTITUTIONS

- Dates: 1 tablespoon agave nectar, coconut nectar, or any other liquid sweetener
- Balsamic vinegar: red wine vinegar or lemon juice
- Zucchini: yellow squash, or 2 (12-ounce) bags kelp noodles, rinsed and drained

COOKED VARIATION

Toss the marinara sauce with cooked whole grain spaghetti instead of spiralized zucchini.

(left to right) Spaghetti alla Marinara (adjacent), Spinach-Walnut Pesto Pasta (page 138)

Spinach-Walnut Pesto Pasta

YIELD: 4 SERVINGS   `CO` `‹30`

Using spinach in your pesto helps trim the cost bit, and walnuts make a great stand-in for pricey pine nuts. (See photo, page 137.)

For the pesto:
1/3 cup dry walnuts
1 small clove garlic, peeled
2 tablespoons nutritional yeast
3/4 teaspoon sea salt
1 bunch fresh basil, stems removed (about 1 cup)
1 1/2 cups packed fresh spinach
1/2 teaspoon lemon juice
2 tablespoons olive oil
2 to 3 tablespoons filtered water
For the pasta:
4 medium zucchini, peeled if desired, spiralized

Combine the walnuts, garlic, yeast, and salt in a food processor and pulse into coarse crumbs. Add the basil, spinach, and lemon juice and pulse until finely chopped, stopping to scrape down the sides if necessary. Add the oil, a tablespoon at a time, pulsing to combine in between each addition. Add water, a tablespoon at a time, pulsing to combine, until desired consistency is achieved. It should be loose and spreadable but not watery.

In a large bowl, toss the zucchini noodles with the pesto sauce. Serve immediately.

Per serving: 163 calories, 13.6g fat (2g sat), 8.5g carbs, 5g fiber, 5.1g protein

SUBSTITUTIONS

- Walnuts: pine nuts or pistachios
- Spinach: 1 bunch fresh flat-leaf parsley, stems removed
- Pesto: 1 batch Basil-Parsley Pesto (page 91) or 1 cup store-bought vegan pesto
- Zucchini: yellow squash, or 2 (12-ounce) bags kelp noodles, rinsed and drained

COOKED VARIATION

Toss the pesto with cooked whole grain spaghetti instead of spiralized zucchini.

Caprese-Olive Bruschetta

YIELD: 8 SLICES   `CO`

This makes a great appetizer, or a light lunch for 2 to 3 people, and is full of healthy raw fats from nuts, seeds, and olives. Make your choice of bread ahead of time, along with some basic nut cheese, and you'll be good to go.

8 slices Nut and Seed Flatbread (page 72) or Rosemary-Garlic Bread (page 66)

1/2 batch Basic Nut Cheese (page 82), preferably made with cashews

1 medium ripe tomato, cored and thinly sliced

1/2 cup pitted Kalamata olives, roughly chopped

1/4 cup fresh basil leaves, thinly sliced

Spread each slice of bread with 1 tablespoon Basic Nut Cheese. Top evenly with the sliced tomato, chopped olives, and basil.

Per slice: 203 calories, 17g fat (2g sat), 9.6g carbs, 6g fiber, 6.4g protein

SUBSTITUTIONS

- Basic Nut Cheese: 8 ounces store-bought vegan cream cheese
- Basil: chopped fresh flat-leaf parsley

COOKED VARIATION

Instead of using raw bread, make the bruschetta with your favorite homemade or store-bought whole grain bread.

Athenian Deli Wraps

YIELD: 6 SERVINGS (2 WRAPS PER SERVING)

Wraps are a great way to use up leftovers, in this case hummus and nut cheese. They're also a raw food favorite because they're so easy and quick to make! The hydrating cucumber and collards in this recipe nicely offset the richer olives and cheese.

12 large collard leaves, tough stems removed

1 1/2 cups Zucchini Hummus or hummus of choice (see pages 110-117)

1/2 large cucumber, peeled if desired and diced

1/2 cup sundried tomatoes, soaked for 30 minutes, drained, and roughly chopped

1/2 cup pitted Kalamata olives, roughly chopped

6 tablespoons Basic Nut Cheese (page 82), preferably made with macadamia nuts, crumbled

1/4 cup chopped fresh flat-leaf parsley

2 tablespoons hempseeds

Spread about 2 tablespoons hummus down the center of each collard leaf, then divide all remaining ingredients among the leaves. Roll each leaf up like a burrito and serve immediately.

Per serving: 196 calories, 15g fat (2g sat), 12.5g carbs, 4g fiber, 6.6g protein

SUBSTITUTIONS

- Collards: Swiss chard or romaine leaves
- Sundried tomatoes: 1 large ripe tomato, cored, seeded, and chopped
- Basic Nut Cheese: store-bought vegan feta cheese or crumbled firm tofu
- Hempseeds: sesame seeds

Almond Butter Sesame Noodles, page 141

Almond Butter Sesame Noodles

YIELD: 4 SERVINGS   `CO` `30`

I've always loved Asian noodle dishes with peanutty sauces. In this raw version, the more subdued flavor of almond butter produces a mild, nuanced sauce that's the perfect match for the fresh veggies and somewhat-crunchy kelp noodles (though peanut butter would be a fine substitute). See Resources (page 228) for info on where to buy iodine-rich, nearly-calorie-free kelp noodles, but if they aren't an option for you, don't fret; I make this just as often with zucchini noodles or even cooked whole grain noodles in their place.

For the almond butter sauce:

1/4 cup Almond Butter (page 92)

1/4 cup tamari

1 tablespoon sesame oil

1 tablespoon rice vinegar

1 tablespoon agave nectar

1 small clove garlic, peeled and minced

1 teaspoon minced fresh ginger or 1/2 teaspoon ground ginger

1 teaspoon sriracha hot sauce (optional)

For the noodles:

2 (12-ounce) bags kelp noodles, rinsed and drained

2 medium carrots, peeled if desired and cut into matchsticks

1 large red bell pepper, stemmed, seeded, and cut into matchsticks

3 green onions, white and light green parts thinly sliced

1/4 cup dry cashews (optional)

2 tablespoons sesame seeds

In a small bowl, whisk together all sauce ingredients.

In a large bowl, combine the noodles, carrot, and bell pepper. Add the almond butter sauce and toss to coat. Refrigerate for 2 hours, until chilled, or serve immediately. Garnish with the green onion, cashews, and sesame seeds just before serving.

Per serving: 265 calories, 19.2g fat (2g sat), 19.8g carbs, 4g fiber, 7.7g protein

SUBSTITUTIONS

- Almond Butter: use a storebought peanut butter
- Tamari: soy sauce, nama shoyu, or liquid aminos
- Agave nectar: coconut nectar or any other liquid sweetener

- Kelp noodles: 4 medium zucchini or yellow squash, peeled if desired, spiralized
- Cashews: dry-roasted peanuts
- Sesame seeds: hempseeds

COOKED VARIATION

Toss the almond butter sauce with cooked udon, soba, or other whole grain noodles instead of kelp noodles.

Vermicelli with Pecan Cream Sauce

YIELD: 4 SERVINGS   CO   ‹30

This unctuous pecan sauce is so inexplicably exquisite, I've found myself enjoying it by the spoonful. (Did I say that out loud?)

For the pecan cream sauce:
1/2 cup pecans, soaked for 2 to 4 hours and drained
1/4 cup cashews, soaked for 2 to 4 hours and drained
1/4 cup Almond Milk (page 30) (preferably unsweetened)
1/4 cup olive oil
2 tablespoons nutritional yeast
2 tablespoons filtered water
1/2 small clove garlic, peeled
1 teaspoon lemon juice
1/2 teaspoon sea salt
1/4 teaspoon ground black pepper
For the vermicelli:
4 medium zucchini, peeled if desired, spiralized
1/4 cup chopped fresh flat-leaf parsley (optional)

Combine all sauce ingredients in a high-speed blender and blend until very smooth. Transfer to a large bowl, add the zucchini, and toss to coat thoroughly. Serve immediately, garnished with the parsley, if desired.

Per serving: 298 calories, 27.6g fat (3g sat), 11.3g carbs, 4g fiber, 6g protein

SUBSTITUTIONS

- Pecans: walnuts

- Cashews: macadamia nuts
- Almond Milk: any other unsweetened nondairy milk
- Zucchini: yellow squash, or 2 (12-ounce) bags kelp noodles, rinsed and drained

COOKED VARIATION

Toss the pecan cream sauce with cooked whole grain spaghetti instead of spiralized zucchini.

Vermicelli with Pecan Cream Sauce (page 142) with Moroccan Grated Carrot Toss (page 175)

Mushroom-Nut Burgers

YIELD: 6 BURGERS   CO

Calling all mushroom-lovers! These burgers are full of the earthy, umami flavor of marinated mushrooms, paired with the omega-3 power of walnuts. The patties look eerily similar to "real" burgers, but they're 100 percent vegan, raw, delicious, and nutritious! Be a raw food rebel sometime and try one on a baked whole-grain hamburger bun.

1 cup dry walnuts
1/2 medium shallot, peeled and chopped
1 small clove garlic, peeled
2 ribs celery, chopped
1 medium carrot, peeled if desired and chopped
1/2 batch Simple Seasoned Mushrooms (page 174)
1 teaspoon lemon juice
1/2 teaspoon ground sage
1/2 teaspoon sea salt
1/4 cup ground flaxseed
4 large butter lettuce leaves
4 thin slices tomato

In a food processor, combine the walnuts, shallot, and garlic and pulse until coarsely ground. Add the celery, carrot, mushrooms, lemon juice, sage, and salt and blend until chunky and combined. Add the flax and process until smooth.

Make It Raw: Scoop the mixture into 6 equal portions on a Teflex-lined dehydrator tray. Shape each portion into a flat, round burger shape about 3/4 to 1 inch thick. Dehydrate for 1 to 2 hours, until the tops look dry. Flip the burgers over onto a mesh-lined tray and dehydrate for 6 to 8 more hours, until dry on the surface but still tender to the touch.

Make It Baked: Preheat the oven to 325°F and grease a baking sheet with coconut oil. Scoop the mixture into 6 equal portions on the baking sheet. Use your hands to mold each portion into a flat, round burger shape about 3/4 to 1 inch thick. Bake for 15 minutes, until the tops are dry, then carefully flip the burgers over with a spatula. Bake for 18 to 20 more minutes, until dry on top and lightly browned. Remove from the oven and let cool slightly before serving.

Serve the burgers on lettuce leaves with the tomato slices.

Per burger: 192 calories, 17.4g fat (2g sat), 7.4g carbs, 3g fiber, 5g protein

SUBSTITUTIONS

- Walnuts: pecans
- Shallot: 1/4 cup chopped red onion
- Flax: finely ground chia seeds
- Butter lettuce: romaine leaves

VARIATION

When you make the half batch of Simple Seasoned Mushrooms (page 174) for these burgers, use 1 large Portobello mushroom cap in place of the 1 cup shiitake mushrooms.

Indian Tartlets with Tomato Chutney

YIELD: 4 SERVINGS   CO

These tartlets, inspired by ones I learned to make at the Matthew Kenney Academy, are an unusual twist on Indian cuisine. They're a little bit like miniature quiches, infused with the aromatic spices of India. The multi-step process does require a bit more time and work than other recipes in this chapter, but that makes the end result all the more special.

For the tart shells:

3/4 cup dry cashews

1/2 cup dry macadamia nuts

1 small clove garlic, peeled

3 tablespoons filtered water

2 tablespoons ground flaxseed

1 tablespoon nutritional yeast

1 tablespoon lemon juice

1/4 teaspoon sea salt

For the filling:

1 medium zucchini, peeled and chopped (1 3/4 to 2 cups)

1 cup cashews, soaked for 2 to 4 hours and drained

1/2 medium head cauliflower, stemmed and broken into florets (2 1/2 to 3 cups)

2 cups lightly packed fresh spinach

1/2 cup fresh cilantro, stems removed

1 tablespoon nutritional yeast

1 tablespoon lemon juice

2 teaspoons good-quality curry powder

2 teaspoons white miso

1/2 teaspoon sea salt

For the chutney:

1 small ripe tomato, cored, seeded, and minced

1/2 small yellow or red bell pepper, stemmed, seeded, and minced

1/2 teaspoon minced fresh ginger

Pinch of sea salt

For the tart shells: Combine all crust ingredients in a food processor and pulse until finely ground. Divide the mixture between four miniature tartlet pans with removable bottoms, pressing firmly and evenly into the pans to create thin crusts. (If the mixture sticks to your fingers, dip your fingertips in a bit of water.)

Make It Raw: Place the tart pans onto a mesh-lined dehydrator tray and dehydrate for 8 to 10 hours or overnight. Carefully remove the crusts from the tart pans, place back on the mesh-lined dehydrator tray, and dehydrate for 1 to 2 more hours, or until completely dry.

Make It Baked: Preheat the oven to 325°F and place the tart pans onto a baking sheet. Bake for 10 minutes, or until dry and lightly browned. Remove from the oven and let cool completely before carefully removing the crusts from the tart pans.

For the filling: Combine the zucchini and cashews in a high-speed blender or food processor and blend until completely smooth. Transfer the mixture to a medium bowl and set it aside.

Combine all remaining filling ingredients in a food processor and pulse several times, until the cauliflower is in small pieces and the spinach and cilantro are roughly chopped. Transfer this mixture into the bowl with the zucchini-cashew mixture, and mix well with a spatula to combine. Divide the filling between the four prepared crusts. (You should slightly overfill the crusts, as the filling will shrink during dehydration/baking.)

Make It Raw: Carefully place the filled crusts onto a mesh-lined dehydrator tray and dehydrate for 6 to 8 hours, or until dry on top.

Make It Baked: Preheat the oven to 325°F and carefully place the filled crusts onto a baking sheet. Bake for 15 to 20 minutes, until filling looks dry. Remove from the oven and let cool slightly before serving.

For the chutney: Toss the tomato, bell pepper, ginger, and salt together in a small bowl. Garnish the top of each tart with a spoonful of chutney, and serve warm or at room temperature.

Per serving: 358 calories, 28.1g fat (5g sat), 21.6g carbs, 7g fiber, 11.7g protein

SUBSTITUTIONS

- Macadamia nuts: almonds
- Flax: finely ground chia seeds
- Zucchini: yellow squash
- Miso: 1/2 teaspoon sea salt
- Bell pepper: mango

VARIATION

Make 1 large tart instead of 4 small ones, extending dehydration/baking time accordingly.

Open-Faced Nutty Butter Sandwiches (page 149) made with Banana Bread Squares (page 68)

Open-Faced Nutty Butter Sandwiches

YIELD: 4 OPEN-FACED SANDWICHES

Matt makes fun of me because I only eat my sandwiches open-faced. He says it's not really a sandwich that way; I say it's even better than a regular sandwich, because you get all the fillings with just half the bread! Have one of these kid-friendly sammies as a snack, or two as a light lunch.

2 tablespoons Almond Butter (page 92)

2 teaspoons agave nectar

1/4 teaspoon ground cinnamon

4 slices Nut and Seed Flatbread (page 72) or Banana Bread Squares (page 68)

1 ripe banana, peeled and sliced

In a small bowl, stir together the almond butter, agave, and cinnamon. Add a teaspoon of water if the mixture is too thick to stir easily.

Spread the almond butter mixture onto the bread, top with the banana slices, and serve.

Per sandwich: 217 calories, 15.5g fat (1g sat), 16.9g carbs, 6g fiber, 6.4g protein

SUBSTITUTIONS

- Nut and Seed Flatbread or Banana Bread: Apple-Cinnamon Raisin Bread (page 70)
- Almond Butter: cashew butter, coconut butter, or peanut butter
- Agave nectar: coconut nectar, maple syrup, or any other liquid sweetener

VARIATION

Omit the cinnamon and banana, and top the nut-buttered slices of bread with Raspberry Jam (page 95) instead.

COOKED VARIATION

Instead of using raw bread, make the sammies with your favorite homemade or store-bought whole grain bread.

Sopes con Mole Poblano

YIELD: 8 SERVINGS   `CO`

Sopes (pronounced "SOH-pehs") are Mexican corn cakes that can be topped with just about anything. I crown mine with a lava-flow of mole poblano, a complex tomato-chile-chocolate sauce. For another pop of color, serve the sopes over a bed of spinach leaves and/or top them with thin, creamy slices of avocado.

For the sopes:

2 cups fresh or thawed frozen corn kernels

1 cup cashews, soaked for 2 to 4 hours and drained

1 teaspoon ground cumin

1 teaspoon sea salt

1 teaspoon lime juice

3/4 cup ground flaxseed

For the mole sauce:

1 cup sundried tomatoes, soaked for 30 minutes and drained

1/2 clove garlic, peeled

1 small jalapeño or Serrano pepper, stemmed and seeded (optional)

2 tablespoons chili powder

2 tablespoons cacao powder

2 tablespoons Almond Butter (page 92)

2 teaspoons olive oil

2 teaspoons lime juice

1 teaspoon ground cumin

1/2 teaspoon sea salt

1/4 teaspoon ground cinnamon

3/4 cup filtered water

To make the sopes, combine the corn, cashews, cumin, salt, and lime juice in a food processor and process until smooth. Add the flax and blend until incorporated.

Make It Raw: Drop the batter in 8 portions onto two Teflex-lined dehydrator trays (4 portions per tray). Use a spoon to spread each portion into a circle about 1 inch thick. Press the spoon into the center of each to create a slight depression. Dehydrate for 2 to 4 hours, until dry on the surface, then flip the sopes over onto a mesh-lined tray. Dehydrate for 4 to 6 more hours, until dry and firm.

Make It Baked: Preheat the oven to 350°F and grease a baking sheet with coconut oil. Drop the batter in 8 portions onto the baking sheet. Use a spoon to spread each portion into a circle about 1 inch thick. Press the spoon into the center of each to create a slight depression. Bake for 10 minutes, until dry on top, then remove from the oven and carefully flip over with a spatula. Bake for about 10 more minutes, until dry and lightly browned. Remove from the oven and let cool slightly before serving.

To make the mole sauce, combine all ingredients in a high-speed blender and blend until smooth. To serve, spoon mole sauce generously on top of each sope.

Per serving: 256 calories, 16.8g fat (2g sat), 23.8g carbs, 7g fiber, 8.6g protein

SUBSTITUTIONS

- Cashews: macadamia nuts
- Lime juice: lemon juice
- Cacao powder: unsweetened cocoa powder or carob powder
- Almond Butter: peanut butter

COOKED VARIATION

Spoon cooked black beans, pinto beans, or vegan refried beans onto the sopes before topping with the mole sauce.

Deconstructed Sushi Bowl

YIELD: 4 SERVINGS

This dish contains all the flavor and nutrition of sushi, but requires only half the effort! Instead of rolling the ingredients into a traditional makizushi, you just toss 'em together in a bowl—no muss, no fuss. If you really dislike seaweed, you can leave the nori off, though it is a fantastic source of essential minerals.

For the sushi "rice":

1/2 medium head cauliflower, stemmed and broken into florets (2 1/2 to 3 cups)

1 tablespoon sesame seeds

1 teaspoon rice vinegar

1 teaspoon agave nectar

1/2 teaspoon sea salt

For the vegetables:

2 medium carrots, peeled if desired and cut into matchsticks

1 large red bell pepper, stemmed, seeded, and cut into matchsticks

1/2 small seedless cucumber, peeled if desired and cut into matchsticks

1 tablespoon tamari

1 teaspoon sesame oil

1 batch Simple Seasoned Mushrooms (page 174)

1 to 2 sheets dried nori, torn into small pieces

2 green onions, white and light green parts thinly sliced

4 teaspoons sesame seeds, divided

Additional tamari, wasabi paste, pickled ginger, and/or diced avocado, to serve (optional)

For the sushi "rice": Place the cauliflower in the bowl of a food processor. Pulse until it breaks down into rice-sized pieces, then transfer to a medium bowl. Add the sesame seeds and mix to combine. In a very small bowl, whisk together the vinegar, agave, and salt. Drizzle the vinegar mixture over the "rice," and toss to combine thoroughly.

For the vegetables: Place the carrot, bell pepper, and cucumber pieces in a small bowl. Add the tamari and sesame oil and toss to coat.

Divide the "rice" between four serving bowls. Top each portion with 1/4 of the vegetable mixture and 1/4 of the Simple Seasoned Mushrooms. Divide the nori, green onion, and sesame seeds among the bowls. Serve with additional tamari, wasabi paste, and/or pickled ginger, if desired.

Per serving: 166 calories, 10.9g fat (1g sat), 14.1g carbs, 5g fiber, 5.5g protein

SUBSTITUTIONS

- Sesame seeds: hempseeds
- Rice vinegar: coconut or apple cider vinegar
- Agave nectar: coconut nectar or any other liquid sweetener
- Tamari: soy sauce, nama shoyu, or liquid aminos

Spanish Garden Paella

YIELD: 6 SERVINGS

I co-created this dish with Chef Cristina Archila (rawfoodartist.com) in culinary school. It was served to diners at Matthew Kenney OKC that night, and it was a hit. Saffron, though very expensive, is a deliciously authentic touch (and has been found to have mood-boosting properties!), but it can certainly be omitted. Feel free to change up the veggies as you please, using whatever's freshest in your area.

For the tomatoes:

1 1/2 cups grape or cherry tomatoes

2 tablespoons olive oil

1/2 teaspoon sea salt

For the "rice":

2 tablespoons hot filtered water

1/4 to 1/2 teaspoon saffron threads

1 large head cauliflower, stemmed and broken into florets (about 6 cups)

1/2 small butternut squash, peeled, seeded, and cubed (about 2 cups)

1 cup dry almonds

1 clove garlic, peeled

1 1/4 teaspoons sea salt

1/2 teaspoon onion powder

2 tablespoons olive oil

1 tablespoon lemon juice

1 teaspoon agave nectar

1/4 teaspoon paprika

1/4 teaspoon turmeric

For the vegetables:

1 small shallot, peeled and minced

1 batch Simple Seasoned Mushrooms (page 174)

1 large red bell pepper, stemmed and seeded, half sliced and half diced

1 cup fresh green beans, ends trimmed, halved diagonally

1 cup (about 18) trimmed asparagus spears, thinly sliced diagonally

In a small bowl, toss the tomatoes with the oil and salt and dehydrate overnight. (Alternatively, bake at 200°F for 1 1/2 to 2 hours.) Refrigerate until ready to make the paella.

In a small bowl, mix the hot water and saffron; set aside. In a food processor, combine the cauliflower and squash. Pulse into rice-sized bits and transfer to a large bowl. In the food processor, pulse the almonds, garlic, salt, and onion powder until coarsely ground, then transfer to the bowl with the rice mixture. Add the olive oil, lemon juice, agave, paprika, turmeric, and the reserved saffron water to the rice and toss to combine.

Before serving, mix the shallot, mushrooms, red pepper, green beans, and asparagus into the rice mixture. Divide between 6 shallow serving bowls, and arrange the tomatoes on top of each portion.

Per serving: 311 calories, 22.2g fat (3g sat), 25.5g carbs, 8g fiber, 8.8g protein

SUBSTITUTIONS

- Butternut squash: additional cauliflower
- Lemon juice: lime juice
- Agave nectar: coconut nectar or other liquid sweetener
- Shallot: 1/4 cup minced red onion
- Green beans: shelled English peas or thawed frozen peas
- Asparagus: snow peas, halved diagonally

Stuffed Peppers with Sunseed Hash

YIELD: 4 SERVINGS   `CO`

These stuffed peppers are filling, thanks to the sunflower seed hash. A dollop of Basil-Parsley Pesto (page 91) on top of each pepper would make a nice garnish.

3/4 cup sunflower seeds, soaked for 2 to 4 hours and drained

1/2 cup walnuts, soaked for 6 to 8 hours and drained

1 small clove garlic, peeled

1/2 cup sundried tomatoes, soaked for 30 minutes and drained

1 tablespoon nutritional yeast

1 tablespoon lemon juice

1 teaspoon ground cumin

3/4 teaspoon sea salt

1 rib celery, chopped

1/2 batch Simple Seasoned Mushrooms (page 174)

2 medium red or yellow bell peppers, stemmed, seeded, and halved lengthwise

2 teaspoons olive oil

Pulse the sunflower seeds, walnuts, and garlic in a food processor until coarsely ground. Add the tomatoes and pulse until incorporated. Add the yeast, lemon juice, cumin, and salt and process until smooth. Add the celery and mushrooms and pulse a few times, until distributed throughout the mixture but still chunky.

Rub each of the bell pepper halves inside and out with 1/2 teaspoon olive oil. Spoon the sunflower seed mixture into the prepared pepper halves, packing it in tightly.

Make It Raw: Place the peppers on a mesh-lined dehydrator tray and dehydrate for 10 to 12 hours, until the peppers are tender and the filling is warmed through.

Make It Baked: Preheat the oven to 325°F and grease a baking sheet with coconut oil. Place the peppers on the baking sheet and bake for 30 minutes, until the filling is hot. Remove from the oven and let cool slightly before serving.

Per serving: 336 calories, 27.9g fat (3g sat), 17.1g carbs, 6g fiber, 9.6g protein

SUBSTITUTIONS

- Walnuts: pecans or almonds
- Lemon juice: lime juice

FEEDING A SMALL HOUSEHOLD

If you live solo or with just one other person, or are the only raw foodie in your house, there may be times when you don't want to make a whole batch of something just for one or two people. Fortunately, trimming raw food recipes down to fewer servings is usually a piece of cake. Unlike in cooking or (especially) baking—where halving a recipe is not always as simple as halving all the ingredients—you can successfully halve (or even quarter) most of the recipes in this book. Simply take care to adjust dehydration (or baking) times as necessary when making smaller batches, and always taste for seasoning as you go along.

One caveat: I don't recommend halving recipes for blended foods (like many of the sauces in the Cheeses, Spreads, & Sauces chapter) unless the original yield size is at least 2 cups. It's difficult for your blender or food processor to work with anything less than 1 cup of food or liquid.

Vegetable Korma Masala

YIELD: 4 SERVINGS   `CO`

Curry...the mere word makes my mouth water. This raw korma may not be totally authentic, but it duplicates the flavors and aromas of traditional cooked curries impressively well. You could serve this with Naansense Bread (page 67) and Mango Chutney (page 90) instead of or in addition to the "rice," and wash it all down with a cooling Mango Lassi (page 40) for a true Indian feast!

For the curry sauce:

1 1/2 cups Coconut Milk (page 31)

1 1/2 cups Almond Milk (page 30) (preferably unsweetened)

1 cup sundried tomatoes, soaked for 30 minutes and drained

1/2 cup cashews, soaked for 2 to 4 hours and drained

1 small shallot, peeled

1 small clove garlic, peeled

2 teaspoons good-quality curry powder

2 teaspoons paprika

1 teaspoon minced fresh ginger or 1/2 teaspoon ground ginger

1 teaspoon lime juice

1 1/2 teaspoons sea salt (or to taste)

1/4 teaspoon cayenne pepper (optional)

For the vegetables:

1/2 small head cauliflower, stemmed and broken into very small florets (about 2 cups)

1 cup shiitake, crimini, or white button mushrooms, cleaned, stemmed, and sliced

1 large or 2 small carrots, peeled if desired and diced

To serve:

1 batch Cauliflower "Rice" Pilaf (page 176)

Chopped fresh cilantro, for garnish (optional)

Combine the curry sauce ingredients in a high speed blender and blend until very smooth.

Make It Raw: Transfer the curry sauce to a large bowl or container and add the cauliflower, mushrooms, and carrots. Warm it in the dehydrator for 1 to 2 hours before serving.

Make It Cooked: Transfer the curry to a medium saucepan and add the cauliflower, mushrooms, and carrots. Gently warm it on the stove over low heat, stirring often, until heated through.

Serve the curry over the "Rice" Pilaf, sprinkled with chopped cilantro, if desired.

Per serving (w/o pilaf): 257 calories, 13.3g fat (5g sat), 31.2g carbs, 8g fiber, 9.5g protein

SUBSTITUTIONS

- Coconut Milk: store-bought refrigerated (not canned) coconut milk
- Almond Milk: additional coconut milk or any other unsweetened nondairy milk
- Shallot: 1/4 cup diced red onion
- Lime juice: lemon juice
- Cauliflower, mushrooms, and carrots: 3 to 4 cups of any chopped veggies you like!

COOKED VARIATIONS

- Add 1 cup cooked chickpeas, 3/4 cup cooked lentils, or 1 cup cubed baked tofu to the curry.
- Serve the curry over cooked brown rice or quinoa.

Vegetable Korma Masala (page 158) with Naansense Bread (page 67)

California Cranberry-Citrus Wild Rice

YIELD: 4 SERVINGS   `CO`

This dish is a study in textures, with chewy wild rice and cranberries, tender citrus fruit, crunchy fennel and almonds, and creamy avocado. The simple orange-scented dressing ties it all together, and its ample doses of fiber and protein will help keep you full for hours.

1 cup wild rice

3 cups filtered water

2 tablespoons olive oil

1/2 teaspoon sea salt

2 medium oranges, peeled and segmented, reserving 3 tablespoons juice

1 medium ripe avocado, pitted, peeled, and diced

1/2 small fennel bulb, very thinly sliced

1/3 cup dried cranberries

1/4 cup dry almonds, roughly chopped

Combine the wild rice and water in a medium bowl and cover with a lid or plastic wrap. Place in a warm dehydrator for 24 hours to allow the rice to "bloom." Alternatively, place the bowl in the oven (making sure it is OFF) with the light on and let it sit for 24 hours. The rice has "bloomed" when it has plumped up a bit and some of the rice grains have opened to reveal the white interior. Rinse the rice thoroughly in a colander and drain it.

In a medium bowl, whisk together the oil, salt, and reserved orange juice. Add the wild rice and toss to coat. Add the orange segments, avocado, fennel, and cranberries and toss gently to combine. Refrigerate for 2 hours, until chilled, or serve immediately. Sprinkle with the chopped almonds just before serving.

Per serving: 387 calories, 17.1g fat (3g sat), 54.3g carbs, 10g fiber, 9.1g protein

SUBSTITUTIONS

- Oranges: tangerines, clementines, blood oranges, 1/2 pomelo, or 1/2 grapefruit
- Fennel: 1 rib celery, thinly sliced
- Cranberries: golden raisins or raisins
- Almonds: pine nuts

COOKED VARIATION

Omit the wild rice and water and skip the "blooming" step, tossing the dressing, fruit, and veggies with cooked brown rice instead.

Fiesta Taco Roll-Ups

YIELD: 6 SERVINGS   `CO`

The nut and seed mixture in the taco "meat" provides a depth and complexity that a single nut can't provide, but that said, feel free to use whatever combination of nuts and seeds you have on hand. Combine the "meat" with Nacho Cheese Sauce, Garden Fresh Salsa, and Garlicky Guacamole, and you'll have a raw taco bar of epic proportions! (See photo, page 134.)

For the taco "meat":

1/3 cup dry sunflower seeds

1/3 cup dry walnuts

1/3 cup dry pistachios

1 clove garlic, peeled

1/2 medium red bell pepper, stemmed, seeded, and chopped

1/4 cup sundried tomatoes, soaked 30 minutes and drained (soaking water reserved)

1/4 cup chopped fresh cilantro (optional)

1 small jalapeño, stemmed, seeded, and minced (optional)

2 teaspoons chili powder

1 teaspoon ground cumin

1 teaspoon lime juice

1/2 teaspoon ground coriander

1/4 teaspoon dried oregano

1/4 teaspoon sea salt

1/8 teaspoon cayenne pepper (optional)

To serve:

1 batch Nacho Cheese Sauce (page 87)

1 batch Garden Fresh Salsa (page 89)

1 batch Garlicky Guacamole (page 88)

1/2 cup fresh or thawed frozen corn kernels (optional)

12 large romaine leaves

For the taco "meat": Combine the sunflower seeds, walnuts, pistachios, and garlic in a food processor and pulse until roughly chopped. Add the red pepper, sundried tomatoes, cilantro, and jalapeño, if using, and pulse until combined. Add the chili powder, cumin, lime juice, coriander, oregano, salt, and cayenne (if using) and pulse until combined. If the mixture is too dry to process, add the sundried tomato soaking liquid 2 teaspoons at a time.

To serve: Serve taco-bar-style by placing the nutmeat, nacho cheese, salsa, guacamole, and corn kernels in separate bowls. To build a roll-up, pile a spoonful of each topping on a romaine leaf, roll, and eat.

Per 3 tablespoons "meat": 144 calories, 11.9g fat (1g sat), 7.2g carbs, 3g fiber, 4.8g protein

SUBSTITUTIONS

- Sunflower seeds: additional walnuts or almonds
- Walnuts: additional sunflower seeds or almonds
- Pistachios: additional walnuts or almonds
- Red bell pepper: 1 small ripe tomato, cored, seeded, and chopped
- Cilantro: flat-leaf parsley
- Nacho Cheese Sauce: 1 batch Mexican Cheddar Cheese (page 83), crumbled, or 1 cup store-bought vegan shredded cheddar cheese
- Garden Fresh Salsa: 1 to 1 1/2 cups store-bought salsa
- Garlicky Guacamole: 1 ripe Hass avocado, pitted, peeled, and diced

COOKED VARIATIONS

- Add 1 cup cooked black or pinto beans to the taco "meat."
- Spoon the fillings into store-bought taco shells or whole grain or corn tortillas instead of romaine leaves.

Primavera Pesto Pizza

YIELD: 8 "PERSONAL PAN" PIZZAS `CO`

Once you try my raw pizza crust, you may never make yours any other way! The inclusion of almond butter is a trick I learned from Russell James; it keeps the crust slightly chewy. You can leave it out if you prefer a crisper, more cracker-like texture, or simply a nut-free crust. (See photo, page 167.)

For the crust:

1 very large or 2 medium zucchini, peeled and chopped (about 3 cups)

1 small clove garlic, peeled

2 tablespoons nutritional yeast

2 tablespoons Almond Butter (page 92)

2 tablespoons olive oil

2 teaspoons lemon juice

1 teaspoon dried basil

1 teaspoon ground oregano

1 teaspoon sea salt

1 cup oat flour

1 cup buckwheat flour

3/4 cup ground flaxseed

For the toppings:

1 batch Basil-Parsley Pesto (page 91)

1 batch Basic Nut Cheese (page 82), preferably made with macadamia nuts

1 pint grape or cherry tomatoes, halved

Freshly cracked black pepper

For the crust: Combine the zucchini, garlic, nutritional yeast, almond butter, oil, lemon juice, basil, oregano, and salt in a food processor or high speed blender and process until smooth, scraping down the sides as necessary. Add the flours and blend again until smooth. Add the flax and blend until well-incorporated. The batter will be very thick and sticky.

Make It Raw: In 8 portions, scoop the batter onto two Teflex-lined dehydrator trays (4 scoops per tray). Using a spoon or small offset spatula (moistened with water), spread each portion into a round crust shape about 1/4 inch thick. Dehydrate for 2 hours, until dry on top, then flip over onto a mesh-lined tray and peel off the Teflex sheet. Dehydrate for 4 to 6 more hours, until firm (though not crisp).

Make It Cooked: Preheat the oven to 350°F and grease a baking sheet with coconut oil. In 8 portions, scoop the batter onto the baking sheet. Using a spoon or small offset spatula (moistened with water), spread each portion into a round crust shape about 1/4 inch thick. Bake for 8 minutes, then flip the crusts over with a spatula. Bake for 7 to 8 more minutes, until dry and lightly browned. Let cool for at least 10 minutes before handling.

To top and serve: Top each pizza crust with 2 tablespoons of the Basil-Parsley Pesto. Scatter the tomatoes evenly across the pizzas. Crumble 2 tablespoons of the Basic Nut Cheese onto each pizza. Top with freshly cracked black pepper, and serve.

Per pizza: 398 calories, 28.1g fat (4g sat), 31.7g carbs, 9g fiber, 11.3g protein

SUBSTITUTIONS

- Zucchini: yellow squash
- Almond Butter: cashew butter or coconut butter
- Basil-Parsley Pesto: 1 batch pesto from the Spinach-Walnut Pesto Pasta recipe (page 138) or 1 cup store-bought vegan pesto
- Basic Nut Cheese: 1 cup store-bought vegan shredded mozzarella cheese
- Grape tomatoes: 1 1/2 cups chopped fresh tomatoes

VARIATIONS

- Make 1 large pizza crust instead of 8 small ones, extending dehydration/baking time accordingly.
- Make 16 mini pizza crusts instead of 8 small ones, decreasing dehydration/baking time accordingly.
- Replace 1 of the 3 cups of chopped zucchini with 1 cup chopped celery, decreasing the buckwheat flour to 3/4 cup.

TOPPINGS

I like to keep the toppings simple with fresh pesto, sweet cherry tomatoes, and crumbly macadamia cheese.

Italian Sausage Pizza

YIELD: 8 "PERSONAL PAN" PIZZAS   CO

My favorite way to eat raw pizza is with impeccably seasoned tomato sauce and flavorful nutmeat "sausage," dotted with rich, creamy nut cheese. This pie also happens to be packed with heart-healthy lycopene (from the sundried tomatoes) and omega-3 fats (thanks to the walnuts), along with a host of other nutrients.

For the crust:

1 batch prepared crusts from the Primavera Pesto Pizza recipe (page 164)

For the pizza sauce:

1/2 cup sundried tomatoes, soaked for 30 minutes and drained

1 small ripe tomato, cored, seeded, and chopped

1 small pitted date

1 small clove garlic, peeled

1 tablespoon nutritional yeast

2 teaspoons olive oil

1 teaspoon ground oregano

1/2 teaspoon fennel seeds

1/2 teaspoon sea salt

1/2 to 3/4 cup filtered water, as needed to thin

For the "sausage":

1 cup dry walnuts

1 small clove garlic, peeled

2 tablespoons tamari

2 teaspoons fennel seeds

1 teaspoon dried basil

1/2 teaspoon dried oregano

1/2 teaspoon lemon juice

1/2 teaspoon crushed red pepper flakes (optional)

To serve:

1 batch Basic Nut Cheese (page 82), preferably made with macadamia nuts

Freshly cracked black pepper

For the crust: Prepare the pizza crust as directed on pages 164-165.

For the pizza sauce: Combine all sauce ingredients, including 1/2 cup water, in a high-speed blender and blend to combine. Add more water, 2 tablespoons at a time, as needed to help it blend smoothly.

For the "sausage": Combine the walnuts and garlic in a food processor and pulse until coarsely ground. Add all remaining sausage ingredients and pulse until well-combined.

To serve: Top each pizza crust with 3 tablespoons of the pizza sauce. Scatter the "sausage" bits evenly across the pizzas. Crumble 2 tablespoons Basic Nut Cheese onto each pizza. Top with freshly cracked black pepper, and serve.

Per pizza: 453 calories, 33.3g fat (4g sat), 33.9g carbs, 10g fiber, 12.6g protein

SUBSTITUTIONS

- Tomato: 1/2 small red bell pepper, stemmed, seeded, and chopped
- Date: 1 teaspoon agave nectar, coconut nectar, or any other liquid sweetener
- Basic Nut Cheese: 1 cup store-bought vegan shredded mozzarella cheese
- Tamari: soy sauce, nama shoyu, or liquid aminos

VARIATION

Replace the "sausage" with your favorite pizza toppings. Try bell pepper strips, chopped olives, sliced mushrooms, diced red onion, fresh basil, or anything else you please.

(top) Italian Sausage Pizza (page 166), Primavera Pesto Pizza (page 164)

Cantonese Veggie Stir-Fry

YIELD: 4 SERVINGS `CO`

Stir fried veggie dishes are the kings of "anything goes" cooking. Of course, here, no frying will occur (unless you want it to!), but the results are the same—lots of crisp vegetables, a complex salty-savory sauce, and plenty of fun add-ins, sprinkle-ons, and accoutrements. Play around to your heart's content.

For the veggies:

1 large or 2 small heads broccoli, stemmed and broken into florets

1 large or 2 small carrots, peeled if desired and thinly sliced

1/2 large red bell pepper, stemmed, seeded, and sliced

6 to 8 shiitake mushrooms, cleaned, stemmed, and sliced

1 cup snow peas, ends trimmed, halved diagonally

1 small clove garlic, minced

1/2 teaspoon minced fresh ginger or 1/4 teaspoon ground ginger

2 tablespoons olive oil

2 tablespoons tamari

1 tablespoon agave nectar

1 teaspoon lime juice

1 teaspoon sesame oil

1 teaspoon sriracha hot sauce (optional)

To serve:

1 batch Cauliflower "Rice" Pilaf (page 176)

2 green onions, white and light green parts thinly sliced

4 teaspoons sesame seeds, divided

For the veggies: In a medium bowl, combine the broccoli, carrot, red pepper, mushrooms, and snow peas. In a small bowl, whisk together the garlic, ginger, olive oil, tamari, agave, lime juice, sesame oil, and sriracha, if using. Pour the sauce over the vegetables and toss to coat well. Add a splash of water if the mixture looks dry.

Make It Raw: Transfer the mixture to a shallow glass pan. Cover and place in the dehydrator to let marinate and warm for 1 to 2 hours before serving. Alternatively, place the bowl of veggies in the fridge overnight to allow the mixture to marinate; serve cold the next day, like leftovers.

Make It Cooked: Transfer the mixture to a large skillet over medium heat. Cook, stirring often, until the mixture is heated through.

To serve: Spoon the stir fry onto mounds of Cauliflower "Rice" Pilaf. Sprinkle each portion with 1/4 of the sliced green onion and 1 teaspoon sesame seeds.

Per serving (w/o pilaf): 157 calories, 9.8g fat (1g sat), 15g carbs, 4g fiber, 4.4g protein

SUBSTITUTIONS

- Broccoli: cauliflower
- Shiitake mushrooms: crimini or white button mushrooms
- Snow peas: sugar snap peas
- Tamari: soy sauce, nama shoyu, or liquid aminos
- Agave nectar: coconut nectar or any other liquid sweetener
- Lime juice: lemon juice
- Cauliflower "Rice" Pilaf: 1 (12-ounce) bag kelp noodles (rinsed and drained)
- Sesame seeds: hempseeds

COOKED VARIATIONS

- Serve the stir fry over cooked brown rice or cooked udon, soba, or other whole grain noodles.
- Add 1/2 cup cubed baked tofu or 1/2 cup cooked shelled edamame to the veggie mixture.

Crunchy Kimchi Wraps

YIELD: 4 SERVINGS (2 WRAPS PER SERVING)   ‹30›

This crisp, energizing snack is full of probiotics, B vitamins, and flavor! It also takes just moments to prepare, and is super low in calories.

8 large endive leaves

1 cup kimchi, homemade or store-bought

1 small zucchini, peeled if desired and diced

1/2 cup dry pistachios, roughly chopped

Spoon the kimchi and zucchini into the endive leaves and top with the chopped pistachios. Serve immediately.

Per serving: 114 calories, 7.6g fat (1g sat), 8.7g carbs, 4g fiber, 5.5g protein

SUBSTITUTIONS

- Endive: 4 large romaine lettuce leaves
- Kimchi: sauerkraut
- Zucchini: yellow squash
- Pistachios: pine nuts, almonds, or walnuts

～ Sides & Snacks

You could call me a serial snacker. If there's anything munchable in my presence, chances are good that I'll pounce on it and have at least a couple of bites. If said munchie is any of the snacks in this chapter, then all bets are off. I can plow through a batch of candied nuts or raw energy bars like nobody's business!

The remaining recipes in this section are side dishes you can serve alongside other meals. Simple Seasoned Mushrooms are a component of many recipes in this book, and Cauliflower "Rice" Pilaf goes great with any curry or stir-fry. Dishes like Moroccan Grated Carrot Toss and Marinated Broccoli and Red Pepper make perfect accompaniments for many of the entrées in the Main Dish chapter.

What's even better? None of these recipes require any advance prep whatsoever! Store all these snacks in the refrigerator unless otherwise indicated.

Build-Your-Own Energy Bars (page 188)

Simple Seasoned Mushrooms

YIELD: 4 SERVINGS ⟨30⟩

You'll see this recipe called for time and time again in other chapters of this book, and with good reason. Marinating your favorite mushrooms will soften them up and infuse them with savory flavor, and they're a cinch to make.

2 tablespoons olive oil

2 tablespoons tamari

2 cups shiitake, crimini, baby bella, or white button mushrooms, cleaned, stemmed, and sliced

In a medium bowl, whisk together the oil and tamari. Add the mushrooms and toss to coat thoroughly. Dehydrate for 15 minutes, or set aside at room temperature for 1 hour, to allow the mushrooms to marinate. Drain any excess liquid off the mushrooms before eating or utilizing in another recipe.

Per serving: 74 calories, 6.9g fat (1g sat), 1.9g carbs, trace fiber, 2g protein

SUBSTITUTION

- Tamari: soy sauce, nama shoyu, or liquid aminos

Moroccan Grated Carrot Toss

YIELD: 8 SERVINGS ‹30›

This little carrot salad contains an amazing array of flavors, not to mention loads of beta-carotene (a precursor to vitamin A) thanks to the carrots. (Photo in background, page 143.)

3 tablespoons olive oil

1 tablespoon lemon juice

1 teaspoon agave nectar

1 teaspoon cumin seeds

1 teaspoon paprika (any kind)

1/2 teaspoon sea salt

Pinch of ground cinnamon

1 pound carrots, peeled and coarsely shredded

1/3 cup golden raisins

1/3 cup green olives, roughly chopped

1/4 cup minced fresh cilantro (optional)

In a medium bowl, whisk together the oil, lemon juice, agave, cumin, paprika, salt, and cinnamon. Add the shredded carrots and toss to coat them with the oil mixture. Add the raisins, olives, and cilantro, if desired, and toss again to combine. Serve immediately, or chill for 1 to 2 hours before serving.

Per serving: 111 calories, 6.6g fat (.5g sat), 13.8g carbs, 3g fiber, 1.2g protein

SUBSTITUTIONS

- Agave nectar: coconut nectar or any other liquid sweetener
- Cumin seeds: 1/2 teaspoon ground cumin
- Raisins: dried cranberries or currants
- Green olives: 1/4 cup capers, rinsed and drained

Cauliflower "Rice" Pilaf

YIELD: 4 SERVINGS   `LF`   `‹30`

Instead of being heavy and chewy like cooked rice, raw cauliflower "rice" has a light texture and a pleasant crunch. Serve it alongside your favorite (raw or cooked) stir fries, curries, and other main dishes.

1/2 large head cauliflower, separated into florets (about 2 1/2 cups)
1/4 cup dry almonds
1/2 teaspoon sea salt
1/4 cup finely diced carrot (optional)
2 tablespoons minced fresh cilantro (optional)
1 teaspoon lemon juice

Place the cauliflower in the bowl of a food processor. Pulse until it breaks down into rice-sized pieces, then transfer to a bowl. Add the almonds and salt to the food processor and pulse until finely ground. Add the crushed almond mixture, carrot, and cilantro to the cauliflower in the bowl. Drizzle on the lemon juice and toss well to combine.

Per serving: 54 calories, 3.2g fat (trace sat), 5.4g carbs, 3g fiber, 2.6g protein

SUBSTITUTIONS

- Almonds: pine nuts or cashews
- Carrot: shelled peas
- Cilantro: flat-leaf parsley
- Lemon juice: lime juice

Marinated Broccoli and Red Pepper

YIELD: 4 SERVINGS   `CO` `<30`

Elegant in its simplicity, this simple side dish will make you forget you ever disliked raw broccoli. For added omega-3 fatty acids, replace half the olive oil with hemp or flax oil. (Photo in background, page 156.)

2 tablespoons olive oil

2 tablespoons tamari

1 tablespoon lemon juice

2 teaspoons agave nectar

1/2 small clove garlic, minced

2 medium heads broccoli, stemmed and broken into florets (about 3 cups)

1 large red bell pepper, stemmed, seeded, and sliced

In a medium bowl, whisk together the oil, tamari, lemon juice, agave, and garlic. Add the broccoli and red pepper and toss to coat well. Add a splash of water if the mixture looks dry.

Make It Raw: Transfer the mixture to a shallow glass pan. Cover and place in the dehydrator to let marinate and warm for 1 to 2 hours before serving. Alternatively, place the bowl in the fridge overnight to allow the mixture to marinate; let come to room temperature before serving.

Make It Cooked: Transfer the mixture to a large skillet over medium heat. Cook, stirring frequently, until the mixture is heated through.

Per serving: 107 calories, 7.1g fat (1g sat), 9.5g carbs, 3g fiber, 3.3g protein

SUBSTITUTIONS

- Tamari: soy sauce, nama shoyu, or liquid aminos
- Agave nectar: coconut nectar or any other liquid sweetener
- Lemon juice: lime juice

Homestyle Applesauce

YIELD: 4 SERVINGS (ABOUT 2 CUPS) `LF` `CO` `‹30`

Making your own applesauce is so easy, there's no excuse not to try it! I use red apples because they're so naturally sweet, but feel free to use green apples—you might just want to up the agave a little bit.

4 large red apples, peeled, cored, and chopped
1 tablespoon agave nectar
2 teaspoons lemon juice
1 teaspoon ground cinnamon
Pinch of sea salt

Combine all ingredients in a high-speed blender or food processor and blend until desired consistency is reached. You can make it as smooth or as chunky as you like.

Make it Raw: Serve the applesauce at room temperature or chill it in the refrigerator for a few hours before serving. Alternatively, transfer the applesauce to a bowl or container and warm it in the dehydrator for 1 hour before serving.

Make it Cooked: Transfer the applesauce to a medium saucepan and gently warm it on the stove over low heat, if desired.

Per 1/2 cup serving: 98 calories, .5g fat (trace sat), 25.7g carbs, 4g fiber, .3g protein

SUBSTITUTION

- Agave nectar: coconut nectar, any other liquid sweetener, or stevia to taste

FOR A CHUNKY TEXTURE
If you prefer a chunky texture, pulse the apple mixture so you don't overblend.

Quick Curried Cauliflower

YIELD: 4 SERVINGS   CO   ‹30

My curry obsession strikes again! Really, though, cauliflower and curry powder were made for each other. They're one of my favorite culinary combos.

- 2 tablespoons olive oil
- 2 teaspoons lemon juice
- 2 teaspoons good-quality curry powder
- 1 teaspoon sea salt
- 1 small head cauliflower, stemmed and broken into florets (about 4 cups)

In a medium bowl, whisk together the oil, lemon juice, curry powder, and salt. Add the cauliflower and toss to coat well. Add a splash of water if the mixture looks dry.

Make it Raw: Transfer the mixture to a shallow glass pan. Cover and place in the dehydrator to let marinate and warm for 1 to 2 hours before serving. Alternatively, place the bowl in the fridge overnight to allow the mixture to marinate; let come to room temperature before serving.

Make it Cooked: Transfer the mixture to a large skillet over medium heat. Cook, stirring frequently, until the mixture is heated through.

Per serving: 82 calories, 7g fat (1g sat), 4.6g carbs, 2g fiber, 1.6g protein

SUBSTITUTION

- Lemon juice: lime juice

Mesquite Candied Pecans

YIELD: 2 CUPS   `CO`

Mesquite powder lends a smoky, almost mysterious sweetness to these nuts. If you don't have mesquite, though, you can just leave it out and make plain maple-candied pecans instead! (See photo, page 182.)

    1/4 cup maple syrup
    1 tablespoon mesquite powder
    1 teaspoon lemon juice
    1/2 teaspoon vanilla extract
    1/4 teaspoon sea salt
    1/4 teaspoon ground cinnamon
    2 cups dry pecans

In a medium bowl, whisk together all ingredients except the pecans. Add the pecans and toss until the nuts are thoroughly coated.

Make It Raw: Spread the mixture onto a Teflex-lined dehydrator tray and dehydrate for 12 to 16 hours, until the nuts are dry.

Make It Baked: Preheat the oven to 250°F and thoroughly grease a baking sheet with coconut oil. Spread the nuts onto the baking sheet and bake for 9 to 11 minutes, stirring once halfway through and taking care not to let them burn. Let cool completely before handling.

Per 1/4 cup serving: 214 calories, 19.5g fat (2g sat), 10.6g carbs, 3g fiber, 2.5g protein

SUBSTITUTION

- Pecans: walnuts or any other nut

Curry-Glazed Cashews

YIELD: 2 CUPS   `CO`

These gorgeous, highlighter-colored cashews combine the inflammation-fighting spice of curry powder with the pleasing sweetness of maple and agave. (See photo, page 182.) These cashews make a great garnish for any stir-fry, curry, or Asian noodle dish.

3 tablespoons maple syrup

1 tablespoon agave nectar

1 1/2 teaspoons good-quality curry powder

1 teaspoon lemon juice

1/4 teaspoon sea salt

2 cups dry cashews

In a medium bowl, whisk together all ingredients except the cashews. Add the cashews and toss until the nuts are thoroughly coated.

Make It Raw: Spread the mixture onto a Teflex-lined dehydrator tray and dehydrate for 24 hours, or until the nuts are relatively dry (they will remain slightly sticky).

Make It Baked: Preheat the oven to 250°F and thoroughly grease a baking sheet with coconut oil. Spread the nuts onto the baking sheet and bake for 9 to 11 minutes, stirring once halfway through and taking care not to let them burn. Let cool completely before handling.

Per 1/4 cup serving: 225 calories, 15.6g fat (3g sat), 18.3g carbs, 2g fiber, 6.5g protein

SUBSTITUTION

- Agave nectar: additional maple syrup, coconut nectar, or any other liquid sweetener

(clockwise from top) Mesquite Candied Pecans (page 180), Baklava Nut Medley (page 183), Curry-Glazed Cashews (page 181), Cocoa-Dusted Almonds (page 184)

Baklava Nut Medley

YIELD: 2 CUPS   `CO`

I don't know about you, but there are times when I'd give anything for a nutty, buttery pastry from my favorite Middle Eastern eatery. On days like those, I hightail it to the kitchen to make these baklava-inspired snack nuts. (See photo, page 182.)

3 tablespoons maple syrup

1 tablespoon agave nectar

2 teaspoons lemon juice

3/4 teaspoon ground cinnamon

1/2 teaspoon vanilla extract

1/4 teaspoon white miso

Pinch of sea salt

1 cup dry walnuts

1/2 cup dry almonds

1/2 cup dry pistachios

In a medium bowl, whisk together the maple syrup, agave, lemon juice, cinnamon, vanilla, miso, and salt. Add the walnuts, almonds, and pistachios and toss until the nuts are thoroughly coated.

Make It Raw: Spread the mixture onto a Teflex-lined dehydrator tray and dehydrate for 24 hours, or until the nuts are relatively dry (they will remain slightly sticky).

Make It Baked: Preheat the oven to 250°F and thoroughly grease a baking sheet with coconut oil. Spread the nuts onto the baking sheet and bake for 9 to 11 minutes, stirring once halfway through. Do not burn. Let cool completely before handling.

Per serving (1/4 cup): 208 calories, 16.5g fat (2g sat), 13.2g carbs, 3g fiber, 5.3g protein

SUBSTITUTIONS

- Agave nectar: additional maple syrup, coconut nectar, or any other liquid sweetener
- Miso: 1/8 teaspoon sea salt
- Walnuts: additional almonds or any other nut
- Almonds: additional walnuts or any other nut
- Pistachios: additional walnuts or almonds or any other nut

Cocoa-Dusted Almonds

YIELD: 2 CUPS   `CO`

These sweet almonds will leave chocolaty fairy dust on your fingers and a big grin on your face. (See photo, page 182.)

- 1/4 cup maple syrup
- 1/2 teaspoon vanilla extract
- Pinch of sea salt
- 2 cups dry almonds
- 4 teaspoons cacao powder
- 2 teaspoons coconut palm sugar

In a medium bowl, whisk together the maple syrup, vanilla, and salt. Add the almonds and toss until the nuts are thoroughly coated.

Make it Raw: Spread the mixture onto a Teflex-lined dehydrator tray and dehydrate for 12 to 16 hours, until the nuts are dry.

Make it Baked: Preheat the oven to 250°F and thoroughly grease a baking sheet with coconut oil. Spread the nuts onto the baking sheet and bake for 9 to 11 minutes, stirring once halfway through and taking care not to let them burn. Let cool completely before handling.

In a small bowl, mix together the cacao powder and sugar. Toss the nuts with the cacao-sugar mixture until uniformly coated.

Per 1/4 cup serving: 171 calories, 12.2g fat (1g sat), 13.1g carbs, 3g fiber, 5.2g protein

SUBSTITUTIONS

- Almonds: hazelnuts or macadamia nuts
- Cacao powder: unsweetened cocoa powder or carob powder
- Coconut palm sugar: brown sugar (not packed), Sucanat, date sugar, maple sugar, or lucuma powder

VARIATION

For Mexican Chocolate Almonds, add 1/2 teaspoon ground cinnamon and a pinch of cayenne pepper to the cacao-sugar mixture.

Road Trip Trail Mix

YIELD: ABOUT 3 CUPS (12 SERVINGS)   ‹30›

Sometimes I simply love spending the day in the car, cruising the open road; just me, Matt, and a bag of this crunchy and addictive (yet mineral- and fiber-rich) raw trail mix.

1 cup dry almonds
1/2 cup dry pecans
1/2 cup dry Brazil nuts
1/2 cup dried cherries
1/2 cup dried blueberries
1/4 cup unsweetened flaked coconut (optional)

In a medium bowl, mix all ingredients together. Store in an airtight container at room temperature.

Per 1/4 cup serving: 161 calories, 11.7g fat (2g sat), 13.7g carbs, 3g fiber, 3.3g protein

SUBSTITUTIONS

- Almonds, pecans, or Brazil nuts: walnuts, pistachios, or hazelnuts
- Cherries or blueberries: raisins, golden raisins, dried cranberries, or other dried fruit

Chewy Pear Chips

YIELD: 4 SERVINGS   `LF` `CO`

These pear chips make a great mess-free snack. They're so low in calories that you could even dip them into a bowl of Vanilla Bean Crème without any guilt (hint hint). Leave the skin on to reap the benefits of pears' high vitamin C and insoluble fiber content.

2 large ripe pears, cored and very thinly sliced with a mandoline

Make It Raw: Arrange the pear slices on two mesh-lined dehydrator trays and dehydrate for 20 to 24 hours, until dry.

Make It Cooked: Preheat the oven to 300°F. Arrange the pear slices on a baking sheet lightly greased with coconut oil and bake for 8 to 10 minutes, until the edges begin to curl. Remove the pan from the oven and carefully flip the chips over with tongs or a fork. Bake for 5 to 7 more minutes, then remove from the oven and let cool completely before handling.

Per serving: 49 calories, .3g fat (trace sat), 12.5g carbs, 2g fiber, .3g protein

SUBSTITUTION

- Pears: apples

SPOTLIGHT ON FATS

Raw food sometimes comes under fire for often containing ample amounts of dietary fats. However, the types of fats you consume matter more than the total amount. Even when raw dishes are rich in fats, they are the beneficial types.

Raw food contains:

Monounsaturated fats, thought to lower cholesterol and benefit heart health

Unrefined polyunsaturated fats, including essential omega-3 fatty acids that promote brain and skin health, reduce inflammation, and lower our risk of heart disease

Medium-chain saturated fats, found to have antibacterial and antimicrobial properties; easily converted into energy (rather than body fat) by our livers

Raw food does NOT contain:

Long-chain saturated fats from animal products, which can raise cholesterol levels and negatively impact heart health

Trans fats, manufactured by hydrogenating vegetable oils (refining polyunsaturated fatty acids to the point that they behave like saturated fats); exceedingly hazardous to our entire cardiovascular system

Also see Cutting the Fat on page 18.

Build-Your-Own Energy Bars

YIELD: 12 BARS   **LF**   **‹30**

Could this recipe be any simpler? I think not! Actually, it's more of an equation than a recipe—just plug in your favorite nuts and dried fruits, and you've just designed your own custom energy bars. See next page for lots of add-in ideas and combination suggestions to get you started.

    3/4 cup dry nuts, any kind
    1 cup pitted dates
    1/2 cup dried fruit, any kind
    Pinch of sea salt

Combine the nuts of your choice and the dates in a food processor. Pulse together until the nuts are finely ground and the dates are well-incorporated. Add the dried fruit of your choice and salt and pulse until combined, chopping the fruit as much or as little as you wish. If you are including any add-ins, pulse them in last. The mixture will be very sticky.

Press the mixture into a wax-paper-lined 8-inch square pan and freeze for at least one hour. Once frozen, cut into 12 bars or squares. Store in the refrigerator or freezer.

Per bar: 112 calories, 5.1g fat (.5g sat), 17g carbs, 2g fiber, 2g protein*

*These nutritional values are approximate due to slight variations in the nutritional content of various nuts and dried fruits.

ADD-INS
Pulse any of the following into the mixture:

  1/4 cup cacao powder, carob powder, or unsweetened cocoa powder

  1/4 cup unsweetened shredded coconut

  1/4 cup vegan protein powder

  2 tablespoons chia seeds, hempseeds, or sesame seeds

  2 tablespoons cacao nibs or nondairy chocolate chips

  1 teaspoon instant coffee granules

  1 teaspoon spirulina or powdered greens supplement

  1 teaspoon citrus zest (lemon, lime, orange, grapefruit, etc.)

  1/2 teaspoon flavor extract (vanilla, almond, hazelnut, etc.)

  1/2 teaspoon ground cinnamon

COMBINATIONS

  Apple Cobbler Bars: walnuts + dried apples + 1/2 teaspoon ground cinnamon

  Cherry-Chocolate Bars: pecans + dried cherries + 1/4 cup cacao powder or carob powder

  Sunny Apricot Bars: cashews + dried apricots + 1 teaspoon orange or lemon zest

  Island Paradise Bars: macadamia nuts + dried bananas + 1/4 cup unsweetened shredded coconut

  Persian Spice Bars: pistachios + golden raisins + 1/4 teaspoon ground cardamom

  Italian Fig Bars: hazelnuts + dried figs + 1/2 teaspoon vanilla extract

  Exotic Holiday Bars: Brazil nuts + dried cranberries + 1/4 cup candied ginger

  Sweet Simplicity Bars: almonds + raisins + 1/4 teaspoon ground cinnamon

  Big Spender Bars: pine nuts + goji berries + seeds from 1/2 vanilla bean

  Hodgepodge Bars: mixed nuts + mixed dried fruit

VARIATION

  Instead of making bars, roll the mixture into snack-size balls.

Rainbow Fruit Salad

YIELD: 4 SERVINGS   **LF** **‹30**

Fruit salad should be a feast for the eyes as well as the taste buds, and this mix fits the bill. Ruby-red strawberries, electric green grapes, sunny orange mango, and blue-purple berries (or any other similarly-hued fruits) create a veritable rainbow of colors and nutrients, all bathed in a zingy-sweet syrup.

For the ginger-mint nectar:
1/4 cup agave nectar
2 tablespoons candied ginger, finely minced
1 tablespoon fresh mint leaves, finely minced
2 teaspoons lemon juice
Pinch of sea salt
For the fruit:
1 1/2 cups strawberries, hulled and quartered
1 cup green grapes
1 small ripe mango, peeled, seeded, and diced
3/4 cup fresh blueberries

To make the ginger-mint nectar, stir together the agave, ginger, mint, lemon juice, and salt in a small bowl.

In a large bowl, toss together the strawberries, grapes, mango, and blueberries. Add the nectar and toss to coat. Chill for at least one hour before serving to allow the fruit to macerate.

Per serving: 164 calories, .5g fat (trace sat), 42.5g carbs, 4g fiber, 1.1g protein

SUBSTITUTIONS

- Agave nectar: coconut nectar or any other liquid sweetener
- Candied ginger: 1 to 2 teaspoons minced fresh ginger or 1/4 teaspoon ground ginger
- Strawberries: chopped seedless watermelon
- Grapes: diced honeydew melon, or 2 to 3 kiwifruits, peeled and sliced
- Mango: 1 cup chopped pineapple, cantaloupe, peaches, or fresh apricots
- Blueberries: blackberries

~ Desserts

||||||||||||||||||||||||||||||||||||||||||||||||||||||||||||||||||||||||||||||||||||||||||

One way to turn someone into an instant raw food fanatic is to introduce them to the world of raw desserts. I know of no better gateway to raw food than delectable chocolates, cookies, brownies, tarts, ice cream, puddings, and other treats like the ones in this chapter. The fact that they are all free of dairy, gluten, refined sugars, heated oils, and animal products is just icing on the (raw vegan) cake. No matter what your favorite dessert flavors are—chocolate, vanilla, caramel, fruit, nut butter, maple, and so on—I've got you covered in this collection of enticing raw sweet treats.

Remember to refer to the Basic Techniques and Guidelines section (page 21) for detailed instructions on how to melt oils and butters, how to make homemade flours, and more. All desserts should be stored in the refrigerator unless otherwise specified...if you end up with any leftovers at all, that is!

Caramel Fudge Brownies (page 204)

Famous Five-Minute Blondies

YIELD: 16 SERVINGS   ▪30

I can't say enough good things about these blondies! The oils released by the ground nuts combine with the succulent dates to make them astonishingly moist, yet they're also nutty and slightly crumbly. The vanilla, sugar, and salt marry seamlessly into a butterscotch-like flavor. You'll really feel like you're biting into a chewy baked dessert. Top with Chocolate Silk Ganache (page 93) for added extravagance!

1 cup dry macadamia nuts

1 cup dry walnuts

1/4 cup coconut palm sugar

2 teaspoons vanilla extract

1/8 teaspoon sea salt

3/4 cup pitted dates

Combine the macadamia nuts, walnuts, and sugar in a food processor and pulse until the mixture is coarsely ground. Add the vanilla and salt and pulse several more times, until combined. Add the dates, 2 to 3 at a time, pulsing between additions until each date is well-incorporated. The mixture will be sticky.

Transfer the mixture to an 8-inch square pan (or similar-sized dish) and use your fingers or a spatula to pack it down tightly. Refrigerate or freeze for at least one hour before cutting.

Per serving: 141 calories, 11.4g fat (2g sat), 10g carbs, 2g fiber, 2g protein

SUBSTITUTIONS

- Macadamia nuts: cashews
- Walnuts: pecans
- Coconut palm sugar: brown sugar (not packed), Sucanat, date sugar, or maple sugar
- Dates: golden raisins

All About Sweeteners

The Great Agave Debate

Within the last couple of years, agave nectar has been increasingly maligned as an unhealthy sweetener. Some folks compare it to high fructose corn syrup (HFCS), thanks to agave's high fructose content. In fact, at around 85 percent fructose, agave actually contains quite a bit more of this type of sugar than HFCS, which is 55 percent fructose. However, fructose (which is naturally found in all fruits—"fructose" = "fruit sugar") is not necessarily a negative thing in and of itself. Our bodies do have to work a little harder to convert fructose into glucose for energy (which contributes to agave's low glycemic index), and if our livers get overwhelmed with too much fructose, the excess is stored as body fat. That said, our bodies can store any excess calories as body fat, not just fructose!

Ironically (and confusingly!), then, high fructose content is not actually the main problem with high fructose corn syrup. Rather, it's the extreme amounts of processing, heating, genetic engineering, and chemical refining it goes through that make HFCS an exceptionally poor choice for a sweetener.

Agave, on the other hand, can be made with minimal processing. There are a number of brands that sell organic, low-temperature evaporated agave nectar produced with only natural (not synthetic) enzymes. As long as the agave is unfiltered, it will also contain helpful prebiotic fibers that feed the beneficial bacteria in our GI tracts. Make sure to do a bit of research on different brands of agave before purchasing, and find one that uses minimal processing methods. Blue Mountain Organics is my preferred brand. If you're watching your fructose consumption, coconut nectar is a wonderful alternative to agave, and can be used in its place in any of my recipes. (See Resources, page 228.) And of course, as with any sweetener, do your best to consume agave in moderation.

Sweetening with Stevia

The only all-natural, calorie-free sugar substitute currently available is Stevia rebaudiana, or stevia leaf. Up to 300 times sweeter than sugar, stevia leaf extract can be purchased in liquid or powdered form. It can be useful for anyone desiring a carbohydrate-free alternative to natural sugars, although its intense sweetness and bitter aftertaste can be a turn-off for some. (See Resources, page 228, for information on my favorite brand of

stevia, NuNaturals.) When sweetening with stevia, always start by adding only the smallest amount possible—literally a couple of droplets of liquid stevia or a tiny pinch of the powdered form—and tasting for sweetness before adding any more (and then, again, adding only a drop or a pinch at a time). I have the most success sweetening with stevia when I abide by the following general guidelines.

- When a recipe contains 2 tablespoons or less of a liquid or granular sweetener, omit the sweetener entirely and replace with stevia to taste.
- When a recipe contains 1/4 to 1/2 cup of a liquid sweetener, reduce the amount of sweetener by one-quarter to (no more than) one-half, adding stevia to taste, as well as a tablespoon or two of water or nondairy milk if necessary for proper texture or consistency.
- When a recipe contains 1/4 to 1/2 cup of a granular sweetener, reduce the amount of sweetener by one-quarter to (no more than) one-half, adding stevia to taste. If necessary for proper texture or consistency, reduce the amount of liquid in the recipe by a tablespoon or two.
- When a recipe contains 1/2 cup or more of a liquid or granular sweetener, I generally do not substitute with stevia.

A Whole-Food Alternative Sweetener

If you're wishing for a completely unrefined liquid sweetener, look no further than date syrup. Dried dates are rich in potassium, fiber, and trace minerals, and even better, they're a whole food! Blend up a batch of this easy homemade Date Syrup for all your liquid sweetening needs. You can replace agave nectar or maple syrup in any of my recipes with an equal amount of Date Syrup. Be aware that it will alter the flavor of the dish with its rich, caramel-like undertones (but you might find you like it even better that way!).

Date Syrup

1 cup pitted dates

1 cup filtered water

Combine the dates and water in a medium bowl. Set aside for one hour to allow the dates to soak and soften. Transfer the dates and water to a high-speed blender and blend until completely smooth. The mixture should be viscous but syrupy; add additional water, 2 tablespoons at a time, as needed to achieve desired consistency. Store in a glass jar in the fridge for up to one week. Use in place of agave nectar or any other liquid sweetener.

Chocolate Almond Butter Cookies

YIELD: 1 DOZEN COOKIES   `CO`

If you like nut butter and chocolate (and who doesn't?), you'll love these brownie-like cookies. If you don't want to dehydrate or bake, just shape them into patties and freeze until firm. Voilà—no-bake cookies!

Wet ingredients:
1/2 cup Almond Butter (page 92)
1/2 cup coconut palm sugar
1/2 cup Almond Milk (page 30)
2 tablespoons agave nectar
1 tablespoon ground flaxseed
1 teaspoon vanilla extract
1/8 teaspoon sea salt
Dry ingredients:
1/2 cup coconut flour
1/4 cup almond flour
1/4 cup cacao powder

In a medium bowl, combine the almond butter, sugar, almond milk, agave, flax, vanilla, and salt, and whisk until smooth.

In a large bowl, combine the coconut flour, almond flour, and cacao powder. Add the wet mixture to the dry mixture. Using a wooden spoon, a sturdy spatula, or your hands, mix the dough until thoroughly combined.

Make It Raw: Divide the dough into a dozen portions. Shape each portion into a flattened patty on a Teflex-lined dehydrator tray and dehydrate for 7 to 8 hours. Alternatively, simply refrigerate or freeze the formed cookies until firm.

Make It Baked: Preheat the oven to 350°F and lightly grease a baking sheet with coconut oil. Divide the dough into a dozen portions, shaping each portion into a flattened patty. Place on the baking sheet and bake for 6 to 8 minutes, until the tops of the cookies look dry. Let cool on the baking sheet for 1 to 2 minutes, then transfer to a wire rack to cool completely.

Per cookie: 134 calories, 7.9g fat (1g sat), 14.7g carbs, 5g fiber, 4g protein

- Almond Butter: cashew butter or peanut butter
- Coconut palm sugar: brown sugar (not packed), Sucanat, date sugar, or maple sugar
- Almond Milk: any other nondairy milk
- Agave nectar: maple syrup, coconut nectar, or any other liquid sweetener
- Flax: finely ground chia seeds
- Coconut flour: additional almond flour (reducing the amount of almond milk to 6 tablespoons)
- Almond flour: any other nut flour or oat flour
- Cacao powder: unsweetened cocoa powder or carob powder

VARIATION

Stir 1/3 cup chopped Raw Chocolate Bar (page 206), 1/4 cup cacao nibs, 1/3 cup store-bought nondairy chocolate chips, or 1/4 cup chopped walnuts into the dough before shaping into cookies.

Crunchy Salted Cashew Cookies

YIELD: 1 DOZEN COOKIES　`CO`　`‹30`

Sweet, buttery cashews form the base for these quick-to-make cookies. Since there's no excess water in the recipe, there's no need to dehydrate—just refrigerate or freeze until firm, and enjoy! When baked, these resemble lace cookies, with crisp-sugared bottoms and chewy centers. Just be sure to let them cool completely on the baking sheet before removing, or else they'll fall apart. (See photo, page 207.)

　1 cup dry cashews
　1/4 cup coconut palm sugar
　1/2 + 1/8 teaspoon sea salt, divided
　1/4 cup agave nectar
　2 tablespoons melted coconut oil
　1/4 teaspoon vanilla extract
　1/4 cup almond flour
　1 teaspoon ground flaxseed

Place the cashews in the bowl of a food processor and pulse until roughly chopped. Remove 1/4 cup of the chopped cashews and set aside. Add the sugar and 1/2 teaspoon of the salt to the food processor and pulse until the cashews are coarsely ground. Add the agave, coconut oil, and vanilla, and pulse until a sticky dough forms.

Transfer the mixture to a medium bowl and add the flour, flax, and reserved chopped cashews. Using a wooden spoon, a sturdy spatula, or your hand, mix the dough until thoroughly combined.

Make It Raw: Divide the dough into a dozen portions, shaping each portion into a cookie shape. Place on a baking sheet and sprinkle evenly with the remaining 1/8 teaspoon salt. Refrigerate or freeze until firm.

Make It Baked: Preheat the oven to 350°F and lightly grease a baking sheet with coconut oil. Divide the dough into a dozen portions, shaping each portion into a cookie shape. Place on the baking sheet and sprinkle evenly with the remaining 1/8 teaspoon salt. Bake for 5 minutes, until the cookies have spread and look brown and bubbly at the edges. Let cool completely (VERY important!) on the baking sheet before moving, handling, or eating.

Per cookie: 129 calories, 8.9g fat (3g sat), 11.8g carbs, 1g fiber, 2.7g protein

SUBSTITUTIONS

- Agave nectar: coconut nectar, maple syrup, or any other liquid sweetener
- Coconut palm sugar: brown sugar (not packed), Sucanat, date sugar, or maple sugar
- Almond flour: any other nut flour, buckwheat flour, or oat flour
- Flax: finely ground chia seeds

White Chocolate-Coconut Fudge Bites

YIELD: 36 PIECES   `‹30`

I will confess, this treat is a bit of a splurge. There's not really any way around using the cacao and coconut butters, since those flavors are the very essence of this blonde fudge. If there's any recipe worth buying them for, though, this is it. (See photo, page 202.)

For the white chocolate:
1/2 cup cashews, soaked for 2 to 4 hours and drained
1/2 cup Coconut Butter (page 92)
1/4 cup melted cacao butter
1/4 cup agave nectar
Other wet ingredients:
1 cup coconut palm sugar
1/4 cup melted coconut oil
1 tablespoon vanilla extract
1/2 teaspoon sea salt
Dry ingredients:
1 cup almond flour
1/2 cup coconut flour

Combine all white chocolate ingredients in a high-speed blender and blend until smooth. Add all other wet ingredients to the white chocolate and blend until smooth.

Combine the flours in a large bowl. Add the wet mixture from the blender and stir until thoroughly combined.

Transfer the batter to a 6- to 8-inch square pan (or similar-sized dish). Freeze for 30 minutes, then transfer to the refrigerator. Remove from the fridge 15 to 20 minutes before cutting and serving. Store leftovers in the refrigerator for up to one week or in the freezer for up to one month.

Per piece: 102 calories, 7.8g fat (5g sat), 8.1g carbs, 2g fiber, 1.5g protein

SUBSTITUTIONS

- Cashews: macadamia nuts
- Agave nectar: coconut nectar, maple syrup, or any other liquid sweetener
- Coconut palm sugar: brown sugar (not packed), Sucanat, date sugar, or maple sugar
- Almond flour: cashew flour or any other nut flour
- Coconut flour: 2/3 cup oat flour

VARIATION

Blend 1/4 cup Irish moss gel (see page 23) in with the wet ingredients for a lighter-textured fudge.

White Chocolate-Coconut Fudge Bites (page 201)

Chocolate-Covered Cookie Dough Truffles

YIELD: 14 TRUFFLES

No-bake chocolate chip cookies? Check. Rich, liquefied chocolate? Check. Put the two together? Heaven. The chocolate coating for these truffles really needs the cacao butter in order to harden properly, but you can try using coconut oil if you don't mind a slightly messier treat. (See photo, page 207.)

For the cookie dough:

1/4 cup finely chopped Raw Chocolate Bar (page 206)

3/4 cup cashew flour

1/2 cup oat flour

1/2 cup dry walnuts, finely ground

2 tablespoons coconut palm sugar

1/4 cup maple syrup

1 teaspoon vanilla extract

1/4 teaspoon sea salt

For the chocolate coating:

1/4 cup melted cacao butter

1 tablespoon agave nectar

1/8 teaspoon vanilla extract

Pinch of sea salt

1/4 cup cacao powder

For the cookie dough: Place the chopped Raw Chocolate Bar in a small bowl and place it in the freezer. Combine all remaining dough ingredients in a large bowl and mix thoroughly using your hands or a wooden spoon until well combined. Remove the chopped chocolate from the freezer and add it to the dough, mixing it in quickly but thoroughly. Chill the bowl of dough in the freezer for 10 to 15 minutes.

Roll the chilled dough into 14 balls and place them on a plate or baking sheet covered with a nonstick sheet or wax paper. Refrigerate or freeze to chill thoroughly while you make the coating.

For the chocolate coating: Whisk together the cacao butter, agave, vanilla, and salt in a small bowl. Add the cacao powder and whisk until smooth. Set the bowl over a small saucepan filled with 1 inch of hot water (or use a double boiler) to keep the coating in a liquid form. Using a candy dipper or two spoons, dip each cookie dough ball in the chocolate mixture, turning to coat completely, then place it back on the nonstick sheet or wax paper. When all the balls have been coated, place the plate or baking sheet back in the refrigerator or freezer for 1 to 2 hours to allow the coating to harden. Store the truffles in the refrigerator for up to one week or in the freezer for up to one month.

Per truffle: 153 calories, 11.2g fat (4g sat), 12.3g carbs, 2g fiber, 3g protein

SUBSTITUTIONS

- Cashew flour: almond flour or any other nut flour
- Oat flour: buckwheat flour
- Walnuts: pecans
- Coconut palm sugar: brown sugar (not packed), Sucanat, date sugar, maple sugar, or 3 tablespoons lucuma powder
- Maple syrup: agave nectar, coconut nectar, or any other liquid sweetener
- Raw Chocolate Bar: cacao nibs or store-bought nondairy chocolate chips
- Agave nectar: maple syrup, coconut nectar, or any other liquid sweetener
- Cacao powder: unsweetened cocoa powder

VARIATION

Forget the coating and just snack on the naked cookie dough balls.

Caramel-Fudge Brownies

YIELD: 16 SERVINGS

These dark, rich brownies are an updated version of the ones that won me the 2011 Hot Raw Chef award from Living Light International. They're devilishly delicious on their own, but when topped with this cocoa-scented, whipped caramel-vanilla icing, they are out of this world. You'll likely end up with more icing than you need—but I'm sure you won't mind. (See photo, page 192.)

For the brownies:
1 cup dry pecans
1 cup dry walnuts
3/4 cup pitted dates
1/3 cup cacao powder
Pinch of sea salt
For the caramel-vanilla icing:
1/2 cup cashews, soaked for 2 to 4 hours and drained
1/4 cup agave nectar

3 tablespoons coconut palm sugar

1 teaspoon vanilla extract

1/2 teaspoon lemon juice

1/8 teaspoon sea salt

1/4 cup melted coconut oil

2 tablespoons melted cacao butter

For the brownies: Combine the pecans and walnuts in a food processor and pulse until coarsely ground. Add the dates, 2 to 3 at a time, pulsing between additions until each date is well-incorporated. Add the cacao powder and salt and pulse until incorporated. The mixture will be sticky.

Transfer the mixture to an 8-inch square pan (or similar-sized dish). Use your fingers to press down and tightly pack the mixture into the pan. Refrigerate while you make the icing.

For the icing: Combine the cashews, agave, sugar, vanilla, lemon juice, and salt in a high-speed blender. Blend briefly to combine. Then, with the machine running, slowly pour in the coconut oil and cacao butter. Blend until the mixture is completely smooth.

Remove the brownies from the fridge and spread the icing evenly on top. Return the pan to the refrigerator for at least one hour. Remove from the refrigerator 10 minutes before cutting and serving.

Per serving: 214 calories, 17.1g fat (5g sat), 16g carbs, 3g fiber, 3.1g protein

SUBSTITUTIONS

- Pecans: additional walnuts
- Walnuts: additional pecans
- Cacao powder: unsweetened cocoa powder or carob powder
- Agave nectar: coconut nectar, maple syrup, or any other liquid sweetener
- Coconut palm sugar: brown sugar (not packed), Sucanat, date sugar, maple sugar, or 1/4 cup lucuma powder
- Cacao butter: additional coconut oil

VARIATION

Frost the brownies with Chocolate Silk Ganache (page 93) in place of the caramel-vanilla icing.

Raw Chocolate Bar

YIELD: 12 SERVINGS

Not only is this a tasty, snackable dark chocolate bar on its own, but when chopped or shaved, it makes an excellent addition to other recipes. I use a blend of cacao butter and coconut oil to cut the cost a little bit, but you can use all one or the other. If you decide to replace the cacao butter with additional coconut oil, keep the chocolate stored in the freezer. (Photo at top, page 207.)

6 tablespoons melted cacao butter

2 tablespoons melted coconut oil

3 tablespoons agave nectar

1 teaspoon vanilla extract

Pinch of sea salt

1/2 cup cacao powder

In a medium bowl, combine the cacao butter, coconut oil, agave, vanilla, and salt and whisk thoroughly to combine. Add the cacao powder and whisk until completely smooth.

Transfer the mixture into chocolate molds or a 9x5-inch loaf pan. Refrigerate for at least 4 hours or freeze for at least 2 hours, until set. Store in the refrigerator for up to one week or in the freezer for up to one month.

Per serving: 104 calories, 9.6g fat (6g sat), 6g carbs, 1g fiber, .7g protein

SUBSTITUTIONS

- Coconut oil: additional cacao butter
- Agave nectar: maple syrup, coconut nectar, or any other liquid sweetener
- Cacao powder: unsweetened cocoa powder

VARIATION

Jazz up your chocolate by stirring in 1 tablespoon maca or mesquite powder, soaked goji berries, cacao nibs, ground coffee beans, or finely chopped nuts before pouring into the molds.

(clockwise from top) Raw Chocolate Bar (page 206), Sugared Doughnut Holes (page 216), Chocolate-Covered Cookie Dough Truffles (page 203), Crunchy Salted Cashew Cookies (page 200)

Cinnamon Crumble Coffee Cakes

YIELD: 6 CAKES

These moist, decadent cakes make a fantastic special occasion dessert, especially when drizzled with Espresso Reduction (page 95) and/or Vanilla Bean Crème (page 93).

Wet ingredients:

1/2 cup pitted dates, soaked for 15 to 30 minutes and drained

1/2 cup maple syrup

1 tablespoon melted coconut oil

1 teaspoon lemon juice

1/4 teaspoon sea salt

Dry ingredients:
1 1/2 cups almond flour
3/4 cup oat flour
1 teaspoon ground cinnamon
For the crumble:
1/2 cup dry walnuts
1/4 cup coconut palm sugar
1/2 teaspoon ground cinnamon
Pinch of sea salt
4 to 5 pitted dates

To make the cake batter, combine the wet ingredients in a high-speed blender. Blend until relatively smooth. Add water, a tablespoon at a time, if needed to blend.

Combine the dry ingredients in a large bowl, then add the wet mixture from the blender. Using your hands, a wooden spoon, or a sturdy spatula, mix the batter thoroughly, until well-combined.

Make It Raw: Divide the batter into six portions. Use your hands to shape each portion into a small (2 1/2 to 3 inch diameter) cake shape on a Teflex-lined dehydrator tray (or use

Cinnamon Crumble Coffee Cake

ring molds to shape cakes). Dehydrate for 4 to 6 hours, until cakes are firm to the touch. Alternatively, simply freeze the formed cakes until firm instead of dehydrating.

Make It Baked: Preheat the oven to 350°F. Divide the batter into six portions. Use your hands to shape each portion into a small (2 1/2 to 3 inch diameter) cake shape on a baking sheet covered with parchment paper (alternatively, use ring molds to shape cakes). Bake for 10 to 12 minutes, until lightly browned. Move to a wire rack to let cool completely.

For the crumble: Pulse together the walnuts, sugar, cinnamon, and salt in a food processor until coarsely ground. Add the dates, one or two at a time, pulsing in between each addition to incorporate. The mixture should be crumbly.

To serve, top each cake with a generous spoonful of the crumble. Drizzle with Espresso Reduction (page 95) and/or Vanilla Bean Crème (page 93), if desired.

Per cake: 430 calories, 24g fat (4g sat), 50.8g carbs, 7g fiber, 10g protein

SUBSTITUTIONS

- Maple syrup: agave nectar, coconut nectar, or any other liquid sweetener
- Almond flour: cashew flour or any other nut flour
- Oat flour: buckwheat flour
- Walnuts: pecans
- Coconut palm sugar: brown sugar (not packed), Sucanat, date sugar, or maple sugar

VARIATION

Blend 1/4 cup Irish moss gel (see page 23) in with the wet ingredients for extra-fluffy cakes.

WHAT'S THE BUZZ ON BEE PRODUCTS?

Some raw foodists choose to include bee products such as raw honey, bee pollen, and royal jelly in their diets; however, these items are not vegan. Whether you elect to consume them or not is a personal choice, but I have avoided including them in this book to ensure that all my recipes are 100 percent vegan.

Raspberry Lemon Mousse Tart

YIELD: 16 SERVINGS

This tart simply sings of spring! The lemon mousse is astoundingly light and flavorful—I suggest doubling the batch and setting half aside to snack on as-is.

For the crust:
1 cup dry almonds
3/4 cup dry macadamia nuts
3/4 cup unsweetened shredded coconut
1 cup golden raisins
1/4 teaspoon sea salt
For the mousse:
1 1/2 cups cashews, soaked for 2 to 4 hours and drained
2/3 cup coconut water
1/4 cup lemon juice
1/4 cup agave nectar
2 teaspoons grated lemon zest (optional)
1/4 teaspoon vanilla extract
1/4 teaspoon sea salt
1/8 teaspoon turmeric (optional, for color)
1/4 cup melted coconut oil
To serve:
1 cup fresh raspberries

For the crust: Pulse the almonds, macadamias, and coconut together in a food processor until coarsely ground. Add the raisins and salt, and pulse until the mixture sticks together when pressed between your fingers. Press into a 9-inch tart pan with a removable bottom (or a pie plate) and refrigerate or freeze to chill completely.

For the mousse: Combine all ingredients in a high-speed blender and blend until smooth.

To assemble and serve: Fill the chilled crust with the lemon mousse. Chill the tart for at least one hour, or until ready to serve. Top with fresh raspberries just before serving.

Per serving: 247 calories, 18.3g fat (6g sat), 20.1g carbs, 3g fiber, 4.8g protein

SUBSTITUTIONS

- Almonds: pistachios
- Macadamia nuts: cashews
- Raisins: pitted dates
- Coconut water: 1/2 cup filtered water plus 2 tablespoons agave nectar
- Agave nectar: coconut nectar or any other liquid sweetener

VARIATIONS

- Replace 1/2 cup of the cashews in the mousse with Irish moss gel (see page 23) for a more airy mousse.
- Divide the crust and filling between 4 to 6 mini tartlet pans instead of using one large one.
- Serve the lemon mousse by itself, topped with a handful of fresh raspberries.

Warm Apple-Walnut Cobbler

YIELD: 9 SERVINGS   `CO`

This date-based, no-sugar-added caramel sauce does double duty by sweetening both the apple filling and the crumbly topping. Use a crisper variety of apple, such as Pink Lady, Jazz, or Honeycrisp, for best results. Serve with Classic Vanilla Bean Ice Cream (page 219) for a nice warm/cold contrast.

For the apples:

3 medium apples, peeled, cored, and thinly sliced

2 teaspoons lemon juice

1/2 teaspoon ground cinnamon

For the caramel:

1 1/4 cups pitted dates, soaked for 15 to 30 minutes and drained

1 cup Almond Milk (page 30)

1 tablespoon melted coconut oil

1 teaspoon lemon juice

1 teaspoon vanilla extract

1/4 teaspoon sea salt

For the topping:

1 cup dry walnuts

1 cup dry almonds

1 teaspoon ground cinnamon

Pinch of sea salt

For the apples: Combine the apples, lemon juice, and cinnamon in a medium bowl and toss to coat.

For the caramel: Combine all caramel ingredients in a high-speed blender and blend until smooth. Reserve 1/4 cup of the caramel mixture and set aside; add the remainder to the sliced apples and toss to coat well. Transfer the apple mixture to an 8- or 9-inch square baking pan (or similar-sized dish) greased with coconut oil.

For the topping: Pulse all topping ingredients in a food processor until coarsely ground. Drizzle in the reserved 1/4 cup of caramel and pulse several more times to combine. Drop the topping mixture by the spoonful over the apples.

Make It Raw: Dehydrate for 4 to 6 hours; serve warm. Alternatively, serve as is, room temperature or chilled.

Warm Apple-Walnut Cobbler with Classic Vanilla Bean Ice Cream (page 219)

Make it Baked: Preheat the oven to 350°F. Bake for 16 to 18 minutes, until the top is lightly browned. Move to a wire rack to let cool slightly; serve warm.

Per serving: 266 calories, 16.1g fat (3g sat), 30.3g carbs, 6g fiber, 5.2g protein

SUBSTITUTIONS

- Apples: Pears
- Almond Milk: any other nondairy milk
- Walnuts: pecans
- Almonds: hazelnuts or pecans

Banana Cream Pie

Banana Cream Pie

YIELD: 1 LARGE PIE (16 SERVINGS)

Prepare to fall in love with banana cream pie all over again. There are no frozen pie crusts or boxed pudding mixes to be found here, though! Instead, get ready for a nutty, almost buttery-tasting crust, potassium-rich banana pudding made with real fruit, and a whipped cashew cream topping. Take it over the top with a sprinkle of crunchy crushed walnuts and a generous drizzle of too-good-to-be-true Chocolate Silk Ganache.

For the crust:

1 cup dry walnuts

1 cup dry macadamia nuts

1/2 cup unsweetened shredded coconut

3/4 cup golden raisins

1/4 teaspoon sea salt

For the cream:

3/4 cup cashews, soaked for 2 to 4 hours and drained

1/2 cup filtered water

2 tablespoons Coconut Butter (page 92)

2 tablespoons agave nectar

1 teaspoon lemon juice

1/2 teaspoon vanilla extract

1/8 teaspoon sea salt

For the filling:

1 batch Just-Like-Grandma's Banana Pudding (page 221), chilled

To serve:

1 ripe banana, peeled and sliced

Chopped walnuts (optional)

Chocolate Silk Ganache (page 93) (optional)

For the crust: Pulse the walnuts, macadamias, and coconut together in a food processor until coarsely ground. Add the raisins and salt, and pulse until the mixture sticks together. Press into a 9-inch tart pan with a removable bottom (or a pie plate) and refrigerate or freeze to chill completely.

For the cream: Combine all ingredients in a high-speed blender and blend until smooth. Chill until pie is ready to assemble.

To assemble. Fill the chilled crust with Just-Like-Grandma's Banana Pudding. Carefully spread the chilled cream on top of the pudding layer. Top with the banana, walnuts, and Chocolate Silk Ganache, if desired, and serve.

Per serving: 288 calories, 21.4g fat (6g sat), 23.7g carbs, 4g fiber, 5.2g protein

SUBSTITUTIONS

- Walnuts: pecans
- Macadamia nuts: cashews
- Raisins: pitted dates
- Filtered water: coconut water
- Coconut Butter: 1/4 cup chopped young coconut meat or 1 tablespoon melted coconut oil
- Agave nectar: coconut nectar or any other liquid sweetener

VARIATIONS

- Divide the crust and filling among 4 to 6 mini tartlet pans.
- Ditch the crust and serve the pudding in wine glasses, layered with the cashew cream, sliced bananas, and Chocolate Silk Ganache.

Sugared Doughnut Holes

YIELD: 1 DOZEN DOUGHNUT HOLES   `CO`

I originally created these doughnut holes as raw gulab jamun, a traditional Indian dessert of deep-fried pastry balls. To serve them Indian-style, float them in a bowl of agave nectar mixed with a drop of rosewater syrup and a pinch of ground cardamom.

Wet ingredients:
1 small apple, peeled, cored, and chopped
1/4 cup coconut palm sugar
2 tablespoons Almond Milk (page 30)
1 1/2 teaspoons ground flaxseed
1/2 teaspoon lemon juice
1/4 teaspoon vanilla extract
1/4 teaspoon cinnamon
Pinch of sea salt
2 tablespoons melted coconut oil

Dry ingredients:
1 cup cashew flour
1/4 cup coconut flour
1/4 cup coconut palm sugar

Combine all wet ingredients except coconut oil in a food processor and blend to combine. Add the coconut oil and blend until the mixture is smooth.

Add the cashew and coconut flours and process until a wet dough forms. Refrigerate the dough for 10 to 15 minutes to allow it to firm up. Place the last 1/4 cup sugar in a small bowl.

Make It Raw: Using two spoons, a cookie scoop, or your hands, roll small scoops of batter (about 1 1/2 tablespoons each) into balls. Roll each ball in the bowl of palm sugar to coat. Dehydrate for 4 to 6 hours, until dry on the surface but still tender to the touch. The insides will remain very moist.

Make It Baked: Preheat the oven to 300°F and lightly grease a baking sheet with coconut oil. Using two spoons, a cookie scoop, or your hands, roll small scoops of batter (about 1 1/2 tablespoons at a time) into balls. Roll each ball in the bowl of palm sugar to coat and place on the baking sheet. Bake for 10 to 12 minutes, turning 1/4 turn halfway through, until lightly browned. Remove from oven and let cool completely.

Per doughnut hole: 123 calories, 8.2g fat (3g sat), 11.9g carbs, 2g fiber, 2.6g protein

SUBSTITUTIONS

- Almond Milk: any other nondairy milk
- Flax: finely ground chia seeds
- Cashew flour: almond flour or any other nut flour
- Coconut flour: almond flour (reducing the amount of almond milk in the wet ingredients to 1 tablespoon)
- Coconut palm sugar: brown sugar (not packed), Sucanat, date sugar, or maple sugar

VARIATIONS

- Blend 2 tablespoons Irish moss gel (see page 23) in with the wet ingredients for fluffier doughnut holes.
- Replace the coconut palm sugar in the dry ingredients with turbinado sugar to add extra crunch to the outer coating.

Almond Butter-Banana Ice Cream

YIELD: 4 SERVINGS LF ‹30

I'm not much of a sandwich person, but one sammy I do love is almond butter with sliced bananas (à la Open-Faced Nutty Butter Sandwiches, page 149). This is my "ice creamed" interpretation of that snack. The miracle of "banana soft-serve" is that you can have homemade raw ice cream in mere minutes!

4 frozen very ripe bananas, broken into chunks
1/2 cup Almond Butter (page 92)
2 tablespoons agave nectar
1/2 teaspoon vanilla extract
1/4 teaspoon ground cinnamon (optional)
Pinch of sea salt

Combine all ingredients in a food processor and blend until smooth and creamy.

This ice cream is best served immediately, but you can freeze leftovers in an ice cube tray, transferring the cubes to a zip-top bag when frozen solid. To prepare the leftover ice cream, place the frozen ice cream cubes in a food processor, let sit for 5 to 10 minutes to soften just slightly, and pulse or process until smooth and creamy.

Per serving: 235 calories, 9.8g fat (1g sat), 37.5g carbs, 4g fiber, 3.6g protein

SUBSTITUTIONS

- Almond Butter: cashew butter or peanut butter
- Agave nectar: coconut nectar, any other liquid sweetener, or stevia to taste

Classic Vanilla Bean Ice Cream

YIELD: 6 SERVINGS **‹30**

Though I'm usually stingy with them, this is one recipe in which I always use a real vanilla bean. In fact, if you have a high-speed blender, you can just throw the whole bean in there; no need to separate the seeds. (See photo, page 213.)

1 cup cashews, soaked for 2 to 4 hours and drained
1 cup filtered water
1/2 cup chopped young coconut meat
1/2 cup agave nectar
Seeds from 1 vanilla bean
Pinch of sea salt

Combine all ingredients in a high-speed blender and blend until smooth. Pour into an ice cream maker and freeze according to the manufacturer's directions.

This ice cream is best served immediately, but you can freeze leftovers in an ice cube tray, transferring the cubes to a zip-top bag when frozen solid. To prepare the leftover ice cream, place the frozen ice cream cubes in a food processor, let sit for 5 to 10 minutes to soften just slightly, and pulse or process until smooth and creamy.

Per serving: 238 calories, 12.6g fat (4g sat), 29.7g carbs, 3g fiber, 4.5g protein

SUBSTITUTIONS

- Water: any nondairy milk or coconut water
- Coconut meat: 1/4 cup Coconut Butter (page 92) plus 1/4 cup filtered water or nondairy milk
- Agave nectar: coconut nectar or any other liquid sweetener
- Vanilla bean: 1 tablespoon vanilla extract

Strawberry Cheesecake Gelato

YIELD: 6 SERVINGS ‹30›

With a full pound of fresh strawberries and only a touch of added sweetener, this gelato seems downright virtuous! The cashews, almond milk, and coconut butter, however, lend it a cheesecake-like flavor and the creamy richness characteristic of true Italian gelato.

1 pound fresh strawberries, hulled

3/4 cup cashews, soaked for 2 to 4 hours and drained

1/2 cup Almond Milk (page 30)

1/4 cup Coconut Butter (page 92)

2 tablespoons agave nectar

1 teaspoon lemon juice

1 teaspoon vanilla extract

Pinch of sea salt

Combine all ingredients in a high-speed blender and blend until smooth. Pour the mixture into an ice cream maker and freeze according to the manufacturer's directions.

This gelato is best served immediately, but you can freeze leftovers in an ice cube tray, transferring the cubes to a zip-top bag when frozen solid. To prepare the leftover ice cream, place the frozen gelato cubes in a food processor, let sit for 5 to 10 minutes to soften just slightly, and pulse or process until smooth and creamy.

Per serving: 211 calories, 14.3g fat (7g sat), 19.3g carbs, 4g fiber, 4.5g protein

SUBSTITUTIONS

- Almond Milk: any other nondairy milk or coconut water
- Coconut Butter: 1/2 cup chopped young coconut meat (reducing almond milk to 1/4 cup)
- Agave nectar: coconut nectar or any other liquid sweetener

VARIATION

Freeze the finished gelato in popsicle molds to make Strawberry Cheesecake Pops.

Just-Like-Grandma's Banana Pudding

YIELD: 6 SERVINGS   `‹30`

When I created this recipe in culinary school, it prompted my instructor Haylee to exclaim "This tastes just like my grandma's banana pudding!" Don't be dismayed if it turns slightly grayish in color once it's chilled. That's bound to happen, since there are no artificial preservatives or food colorings. Just slice some fresh ripe bananas on top, and no one will notice— they'll be too busy saying "mmm"! (See photo, page 214.)

2 medium very ripe bananas, peeled

3/4 cup cashews, soaked for 2 to 4 hours and drained

1/4 cup Coconut Butter (page 92)

1/4 cup filtered water

2 tablespoons agave nectar

2 teaspoons lemon juice

1 teaspoon vanilla extract

1/4 teaspoon sea salt

Combine all ingredients in a high-speed blender and blend until smooth. Transfer the mixture to a bowl or container and refrigerate for at least 1 to 2 hours before serving. To prevent a skin from forming on the surface of the pudding, refrigerate with a piece of plastic wrap pressed directly on the surface, if desired.

Per serving: 219 calories, 14g fat (7g sat), 22.5g carbs, 4g fiber, 4.3g protein

SUBSTITUTIONS

- Coconut Butter: 1/2 cup chopped young coconut meat (reducing water to 2 tablespoons)
- Filtered water: coconut water or any nondairy milk
- Agave nectar: coconut nectar, any other liquid sweetener, or stevia to taste

PUDDING COLOR

Because there are no preservatives, the pudding may turn slightly grayish in color once chilled.

Spiced "Pumpkin" Spooncream

YIELD: 6 SERVINGS   `‹30`

What on earth is spooncream? I don't know; I made it up! It's thinner than a pudding but denser than a mousse. Carrots make a beautiful raw stand-in for actual pumpkin when paired with all the right spices. This cream is like unbaked pie filling you eat with a spoon! Serve it in wine or martini glasses for an impressive presentation.

3/4 cup cashews, soaked for 2 to 4 hours and drained

2/3 cup filtered water

2 medium carrots, peeled and chopped

1/2 cup maple syrup

2 teaspoons pumpkin pie spice

1/2 teaspoon vanilla extract

1/4 teaspoon sea salt

1/4 cup melted coconut oil

Combine all ingredients except coconut oil in a high-speed blender and blend until smooth. With the machine running, slowly stream in the coconut oil and blend until completely smooth. Transfer the mixture to a bowl or container and refrigerate for several hours or overnight before serving.

Per serving: 222 calories, 14.4g fat (9g sat), 23.3g carbs, 1.5g fiber, 2.3g protein

SUBSTITUTIONS

- Filtered water: coconut water or any nondairy milk
- Maple syrup: agave nectar, coconut nectar, or any other liquid sweetener
- Carrots: 1/2 cup fresh or canned pumpkin purée
- Pumpkin pie spice: 1 teaspoon ground cinnamon plus a pinch of ground nutmeg

VARIATION

Make Pumpkin Ice Cream by pouring the spooncream into an ice cream maker and freezing according to the manufacturer's directions.

Coconut "Rice" Pudding

YIELD: 8 SERVINGS   `LF` `‹30`

Not only is it quicker to make "rice" pudding with chia seeds, it's healthier! Get your omega-3s while indulging your sweet tooth at the same time with this surprisingly low-cal treat.

1 cup cashews, soaked for 2 to 4 hours and drained
1 cup chopped young coconut meat
1 cup coconut water
1/2 cup filtered water
1/2 cup agave nectar
2 teaspoons lemon juice
1 teaspoon vanilla extract
1/4 teaspoon ground cinnamon
1/8 teaspoon sea salt
Pinch of ground cardamom (optional)
1/2 cup white chia seeds

Combine all ingredients except chia seeds in a high-speed blender and blend until smooth. Transfer the mixture to a bowl or container, add the chia seeds, and stir thoroughly to combine. Refrigerate for at least 2 to 4 hours before serving to allow the pudding to thicken.

Per 1/2 cup serving: 151 calories, 6.1g fat (4g sat), 23.7g carbs, 2g fiber, 2.2g protein

SUBSTITUTIONS

- Coconut meat: 1/2 cup Coconut Butter (page 92) plus 1/2 cup filtered water
- Coconut water: any nondairy milk, or filtered water plus 1 tablespoon agave nectar
- Agave nectar: coconut nectar or any other liquid sweetener
- White chia seeds: regular (black) chia seeds

VARIATIONS

- Replace 1/2 cup of the cashews with Irish moss gel (see page 23) for a lighter pudding.
- Make Indian-style kheer by stirring in 1/4 cup dry cashews or pistachios and 1/2 cup golden raisins before refrigerating.

Menus & Resources

This short but important chapter provides menus of *Practically Raw* recipes that go well together as a meal. You'll find a variety of international menus, including all-American, Mexican, Indian, Italian, and Middle Eastern. Additional menus are included for a pizza night, a picnic, a brunch, and a wine and "cheese" night. There's even a "Liquid Diet for a Day" plan, since feeding your body easily-to-digest blended foods for a day can be a great way to detoxify and give your GI system a little TLC if you've spent years on a heavier, cooked-food diet.

Immediately following the menus is a list of sources and resources for finding raw food related items and other helpful information.

↶ Menus ↷

These themed menus offer some suggestions to help you put together fun and flavorful raw feasts. Feel free to mix and match or create your own menu plans.

Mexican Fiesta

Hemp Horchata (page 41)

Fiesta Taco Roll-Ups (page 162), served taco-bar style with:
    Garlicky Guacamole (page 88)
    Nacho Cheese Sauce (page 87)
    Garden Fresh Salsa (page 89)
    Zesty Corn Tortilla Chips (page 78)

Indian Soirée

Mango Lassi (page 40)

Vegetable Korma Masala (page 158)

Cauliflower "Rice" Pilaf (page 176)

Naansense Bread (page 67)

Mango Chutney (page 90)

Coconut Rice Pudding (page 223)

Italian Family Dinner

Insalata di Trattoria (page 131)

Rosemary-Garlic Bread (page 66)

Spaghetti alla Marinara (page 136) and/or Spinach-Walnut Pesto Pasta (page 138)

Marinated Broccoli and Red Pepper (page 177)

Raspberry Lemon Mousse Tart (page 210)

All-American Chow

Your favorite kale chips (page 97)

Mushroom-Nut Burgers (page 144)

Warm Apple-Walnut Cobbler (page 212)

Classic Vanilla Bean Ice Cream (page 219)

Middle East Feast

Your favorite hummus (one or more) (page 109)

Nut and Seed Flatbread (page 72)

Greek Taverna Salad (page 132)

Moroccan Grated Carrot Toss (page 175)

Athenian Deli Wraps (page 139)

Baklava Nut Medley (page 183)

Pizza Night

Rosemary-Garlic Bread (page 66)

Primavera Pesto Pizza (page 164)

Italian Sausage Pizza (page 166)

Sugared Doughnut Holes (page 216)

Picnic al Fresco

Rainbow Fruit Salad (page 190)

Caprese-Olive Bruschetta (page 139)

Open-Faced Nutty Butter Sandwiches (page 149)

Chilled Watermelon Soup (page 123)

Graham Crackers (page 77) or Apple-Cinnamon Raisin Bread (page 70) with
    Coconut Butter (page 92) and Raspberry Jam (page 95)

Brunch Buffet

Cold-Pressed Café au Lait (page 55)

Le Matin Parfait (page 49)

Morning Mushroom Scramble (page 53)

Flaxjacks with Miso-Maple Butter (page 58) and/or Parisian Street
    Crêpes (page 61)

Biscuits and Sausage Gravy (page 62)

Wine & Cheese Party

Olive Tapenade-Stuffed Cheese (page 84)

Balsamic-Fig Pistachio Cheese (page 85)

Christmas Cheese Ball (page 86)

Basic Flax Crackers (page 75) or Nut and Seed Flatbread (page 72)

Chewy Pear Chips (page 186)

Your favorite candied nuts (pages 180-184)

Your favorite wines

Liquid Diet for a Day

Your favorite milks and smoothies (page 29)

Coconut Yogurt (page 50)

Your favorite soups (page 120-126)

Homestyle Applesauce (page 178)

Just-Like-Grandma's Banana Pudding (page 221)

Spiced Pumpkin Spooncream (page 222)

⋙ Resources ⋘

This list of raw-friendly companies is by no means exhaustive, but the companies and sources that follow are my own preferences and recommendations for acquiring ingredients, equipment, or supplements, and for finding educational resources.

Ingredients

Blue Mountain Organics. 100% organic and truly-raw nuts and seeds, nut and seed butters, sweeteners, dried fruit, coconut products, flours, oats, cacao products, superfoods, sea vegetables, prepared raw snacks, and more, all of superior quality and integrity. My #1 go-to source for raw food ingredients. www.bluemountainorganics.com

Nuts Online. Bulk quantities of organic raw nuts, seeds, dried fruit, flours, superfood powders, and more. Large selection, great prices, and fast shipping. www.nutsonline.com

NuNaturals Stevia. The best-tasting stevia extracts and powders I've ever found. Their Pure Liquid Vanilla Stevia is my favorite. www.nunaturals.com

Coconut Secret. The only source, currently, for raw organic coconut nectar; they also carry coconut sugar, flour, vinegar, and aminos. www.coconutsecret.com

Nutiva. Organic coconut oil and "manna" (butter), chia and hempseeds, hemp oil and protein powder. www.nutiva.com

Artisana. Raw organic nut butters, coconut butter, and tahini. www.artisanafoods.com

Sea Tangle Noodle Company. Nutritious, low-calorie kelp noodles. www.kelpnoodles.com

BlueBonnet. Dairy-free probiotic powder. www.bluebonnetnutrition.com

Equipment

Vitamix. My high-speed blender of choice. It's worth the price, as it will last a lifetime. www.vitamix.com

Excalibur. My preferred brand of dehydrators. I like the models with built-in timers and temperature controls. www.excaliburdehydrator.com

Cuisinart. High-quality food processors, ice cream makers, and more. www.cuisinart.com

Paderno World Cuisine. Their Spiral Vegetable Slicer is an excellent spiralizer for making raw pastas. (I recommend purchasing it from amazon.com.) www. world-cuisine.com

Pure Joy Planet. Nut milk bags with free shipping. www.purejoyplanet.com

Supplements

Vega. High-quality plant-based meal replacement shakes, protein powders, and other active lifestyle supplements created by vegan Ironman triathlete Brendan Brazier. www.myvega.com

Living Harvest. Organic hemp protein powders. www.livingharvest.com

Sunwarrior. Raw, sprouted, whole grain brown rice protein and greens powders. www.sunwarrior.com

Garden of Life. Raw vitamin and mineral supplements and protein, greens, and meal replacement powders. www.gardenoflife.com

Education

Matthew Kenney Academy. My "rawlma mater" is the culinary academy of chef Matthew Kenney, my mentor and longtime inspiration. Their classical approach to teaching the art of gourmet living cuisine is unmatched. www.kenneycuisine.com/academy

Russell James. As the UK's leading raw chef and my former instructor at the Matthew Kenney Academy, Russell is an expert on all things raw. He offers online chef courses and learn-at-home DVDs. www.therawchef.com

Living Light Culinary Arts Institute. Cherie Soria's Living Light is the longest-running raw chef school in the country. Their classes are especially well-suited for anyone interested in becoming a raw food teacher or instructor. www.rawfoodchef.com

Drs. Rick and Karin Dina, D.C. I earned my nutrition educator certification from the Dinas at Living Light. Their wealth of knowledge on the science of raw food nutrition is without rival. www.rawfoodeducation.com

Additional Information

Almost Vegan. My blog is the place where you can find out what I'm up to, check out new recipes as I create them, read about my vegan traveling adventures, say hello or ask a question, and generally interact with me!

You can even subscribe to receive my posts by email: www.almostveganchef.com.

Feel free to follow me on Facebook and Twitter as well: www.facebook.com/almostvegan and www.twitter.com/almostveganchef

Acknowledgments

First and foremost, I'd like to thank my publisher, Jon Robertson, at Vegan Heritage Press. Without your extensive expertise in publishing and marketing, this beautiful book would not have been possible. Throughout this whole new-to-me process, you have been endlessly patient and responsive, and as a result, together we've created the cookbook of my dreams. Hopefully it's only the first of many to come!

Thank you to Matthew Kenney, my mentor and longtime inspiration, for your huge role in catapulting me towards making raw food not just my passion, but my career. To Russell James and Haylee Otto, my instructors at the Matthew Kenney Academy, for all the culinary skill and proficiency you passed on to me. To Drs. Rick and Karin Dina at the Living Light Culinary Arts Institute; you reinforced my nutrition knowledge base like no one else ever has. To my recipe testers, for your generous dedication of time and resources to help me make this book the best it can be. Samantha Robertson, Rachel Detwieler, Lisa Pitman, Merryn Ironmonger, Jennifer Marie Smith Robertson, Billie Brockwell, Nicholas Wozniak, and Christine Borosh, thank you for all your hard work.

Thank you to Stephen Melvin, my talented photographer, for helping me get comfortable in front of a camera and capturing the photos of me throughout this book. Thanks also to Geri at Portfolio Kitchen & Home and Lloyd at Doolittle Distributing Inc. for the use of your lovely kitchen spaces.

Thank you to my parents, Ken and Cheryl Ford, for your lifetime of supporting and believing in me. You were an integral part of this accomplishment.

Thank you to my wonderful husband Matt Crawley, not only for helping me eat all this food and do all these dishes (!), but for the immeasurable love and mirth you bring to my life every single day. You offer guidance when I'm lost, you motivate me when I'm down, you encourage me when I'm unsure, and you always know how to put a smile on my face. I truly couldn't have done this without you.

Last but not least, a huge thank you to all my fans and blog readers of almostveganchef.com. Without your thoughtful comments and feedback, often witty and hilarious repartee (Hannah, I'm lookin' at you!), and continuous support and encouragement, I wouldn't be the chef I am today. Thank you all!

About the Author

Amber Shea Crawley is a linguist, author, and chef specializing in healthful vegan and raw food. She was trained in the art of gourmet living cuisine at the world-renowned Matthew Kenney Academy, graduating in 2010 as a certified raw and vegan chef. In 2011, she earned her Nutrition Educator certification at the Living Light Culinary Arts Institute. Amber lives with her husband Matt in Kansas City, Missouri and blogs at AlmostVeganChef.com.

Index

Also Published by Vegan Heritage Press

Vegan Heritage Press is an independent book publishing company dedicated to publishing cookbooks and other publications and products that promote healthful living and respect for all life. Our goal is to bring to the marketplace innovative vegan cooking ideas that will delight longtime vegans, inspire newcomers, and intrigue the curious who want to improve their health and the world in general by cooking excellent plant-based foods.

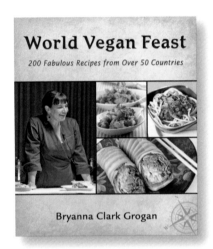

World Vegan Feast

175 Homestyle Recipes from 38 Countries

BRYANNA CLARK GROGAN

Leading vegan cooking expert Bryanna Clark Grogan shares recipes from her vast knowledge of international cuisines.

Developed over years of travel and research, these recipes include many exciting dishes that you won't find anywhere else. They cover comfort foods and munchies; grain and vegetable mains; "meats of the field"; sandwiches, soups, desserts, and an international bread sampler.

The book contains helpful sidebars and tips, as well as helpful menu suggestions.

Paperback, 272 pages, 36 color photos. ISBN: 978-0-9800131-4-6, $19.95.

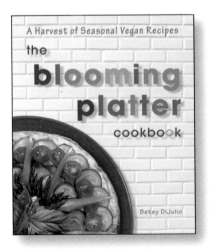

The Blooming Platter Cookbook

A Harvest of Seasonal Vegan Recipes

BETSY DIJULIO

Whether you enjoy your vegan recipes simple or sophisticated, you'll find them in this excellent cookbook.

The Blooming Platter Cookbook is a celebration of the seasons, featuring a wide range of accessible, elegant vegan recipes for the home cook. Spanning regional American favorites and global cuisines, these 175 recipes feature all the essential goodness that fresh vegetables, fruits, and herbs bring to your table, all year 'round.

The book includes recipes for appetizers, soups, sandwiches, salads, main dishes, side dishes, desserts, and brunch, and they are divided by season within each chapter.

Paperback, 224 pages, 36 color photos, ISBN: 978-0-9800131-3-9, $18.95.

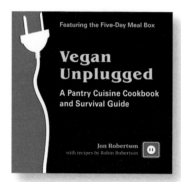

Vegan Unplugged

A Pantry Cuisine Cookbook and Survival Guide

JON ROBERTSON WITH RECIPES BY ROBIN ROBERTSON

Vegan Unplugged is your go-to source for gourmet pantry cooking. Make tasty meals whenever the power goes out from storms, hurricanes, and blackouts. These easy recipes can be made in fifteen minutes or less. This makes the book ideal for camping, boating, or anytime you just don't feel like cooking.

This book is a "must have" for anyone who wants to be ready for anything with great-tasting, nutritious pantry cuisine.

Paperback, 216 pages, ISBN: 978-0-9800131-2-2, $14.95.

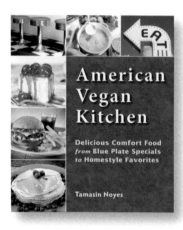

American Vegan Kitchen

Delicious Comfort Food from Blue Plate Specials
to Homestyle Favorites

TAMASIN NOYES

Do you ever crave the delicious comfort foods served at your local diner, deli, or neighborhood cafe? This cookbook shows you how to make vegan versions of your favorite dishes in your own home kitchen.

These 200+ recipes will satisfy vegans and non-vegans alike with deli sandwiches, burgers and fries, mac and cheese, pasta, pizza, omelets, pancakes, soups and salads, casseroles, and desserts. Enjoy truly great American flavors from tempting ethnic dishes to the homestyle comfort foods of the heartland.

Paperback, 232 pages, ISBN: 978-0-9800131-1-5, $18.95.

Vegan Fire & Spice

200 Sultry and Savory Global Recipes

ROBIN ROBERTSON

Take a trip around the world with delicious, mouthwatering vegan recipes ranging from mildly spiced to nearly incendiary. Explore the spicy cuisines of the U.S., South America, Mexico, the Caribbean, Europe, Africa, the Middle East, India, and Asia with Red-Hot White Bean Chili, Jambalaya, Szechuan Noodle Salad, Vindaloo Vegetables, and more.

Organized by global region, this book gives you 200 inventive and delicious, 100% vegan recipes for easy-to-make international dishes, using readily available ingredients. Best of all, you can adjust the heat yourself and enjoy these recipes hot – or not.

Paperback, 268 pages, ISBN: 978-0-9800131-0-8, $18.95.

The recipes on offer here are exciting and flexible, and you'll also find they are very doable for even the most novice cook. With money-saving tips, nutrition advice, information on special ingredients, equipment and techniques, pantry lists, and directions for cooked options, this book is a wonderful entry into enjoying the raw food lifestyle...practically.

—Russell James, The Raw Chef

Beautiful and immensely helpful. The perfect cookbook for omnivores leaning toward veganism, as well as vegans leaning toward raw foods.

—Vegan.com

For anyone wanting to become more comfortable and familiar with the charms and benefits of a plant-based diet, look no further than *Practically Raw.*

—Matthew Kenney, founder of the Matthew Kenney Academy, from the Foreword

Amber's approachable style to eating raw makes it easy for anyone to start making raw foods in their kitchen. Her recipes are inventive, balancing both raw and cooked foods, with an emphasis on health but never sacrificing taste. You'll find the recipes in *Practically Raw* are deliciously divine.

—Christy Morgan, The Blissful Chef, author of *Blissful Bites*

Amber's easy-to-follow recipes make this healthful cuisine easy, joyfully approachable, and a veritable feast for the palate. Whether you're a raw food neophyte or have been enjoying this healthy lifestyle for years, Amber's fresh perspective is nothing less than "rawsome." Her Cocoa Corruption Smoothie is addictive.

—Dynise Balcavage, author of *Celebrate Vegan* and *Urban Vegan*

It's a raw food free-for-all! Amber takes the stress out of uncooked preparations, making delicious results accessible to everyone. Guiding cooks through the world of raw vegan food with gentle instructions and helpful hints all along the way, you 'll want to get into the kitchen as soon as you open the cover.

—Hannah Kaminsky, author of *My Sweet Vegan* and *Vegan Desserts*

I have been impressed with every single recipe in this book I tried. *Practically Raw* is a book for anyone who likes to eat good food that doesn't take forever to make. I would recommend it to every person interested in adding more raw and vegan foods into their lives.

—Eva Rawposa, Uncooking101.com and founder of The Uncooking School